BRIDGING THE GAP

Has the Church failed the Poor?

The Kerr Lectures 1987

John Harvey

THE SAINT ANDREW PRESS: EDINBURGH

First published in 1987 by
THE SAINT ANDREW PRESS
121 George Street, Edinburgh EH2 4YN

British Library Cataloguing in Publication Data
Harvey, John, *1937-*
Bridging the Gap: Has the Church failed the Poor?
—(The Kerr Lectures; 1987)
1. Liberation theology—Great Britain
I. Title   II. Series
261.8   BT83.57

ISBN 0-7152-0607-9

Printed in Great Britain by Bell and Bain Ltd., Glasgow.
Typeset by Print Origination, Formby, Liverpool L37 8EG

BRIDGING THE GAP

Contents

Author's note and acknowledgments

Among the many people I have to thank for their help in the writing of this book, I would like to mention in particular:

—the Trustees of the Kerr Lectureship, for inviting me to give the lectures on which this book is based;

—the Faculty of Divinity of Glasgow University, and its Dean, Dr Joe Houston, for giving me a place in which to prepare the lectures, and advice and encouragement on the way;

—the Presbytery of Glasgow, the Kirk Session of Govan Old, and my colleagues in the ministry, for giving me the time off for preparing them;

—Mrs Emma Roberton for very kindly typing out the final version, and The Saint Andrew Press for their enthusiastic adoption of the lectures for publication;

—my family, for their encouragement and understanding while the work was being done, and especially our daughter Susie for her help in preparing the lectures for publication; and

—Ron Ferguson, Leader of the Iona Community, for kindly agreeing to write the Preface.

The debt I owe to hundreds, if not thousands, of people both in and out of the Church will be obvious in the pages of the book.

People on pilgrimage, from Chaucer's day to ours, have told each other stories, not just to pass the time, but also to encourage each other on the way. And as the stories are told, the point of the pilgrimage, and even perhaps the nature of the true destination, become clearer, bit by bit. If this book can serve, in some small way, as rations for the pilgrim people of God, then I will be happy — and so, I hope, will be the people whose stories I have partly told. I would like the royalties from this book to go towards the Macleod Centre on Iona, the Iona Community's new international centre, for youth and for others, committed to the Gospel imperatives of justice, peace and understanding.

This book is dedicated, with love and gratitude, to my father, Leslie Harvey, and my father-in-law, Hugh Douglas, both of whom died within a week of my beginning to prepare the lectures.

> 'Those who trust in the Lord for help
> will find their strength renewed.
> They will rise on wings like eagles;
> they will run and not get weary;
> they will walk and not grow weak.'

(Isa. 40:31 GNB)

John Harvey
Govan, 1986–87

Preface

What we are seeing in the great housing schemes and decaying inner city areas of Scotland is the virtual end of the Protestant line.

Despite the countervailing mythology, it looks like being the end of the Roman Catholic line too, only later.

The people in what have been described as the Urban Sowetos, the tribal homelands of the disposable poor in Scotland, are not gospel-greedy: at least not in the church's terms. There never was a time when the church attracted the urban masses, but the figures are now so stark that there is no longer point in preference of wishful thinking. The Emperor's threadbare clothes were last seen at the nearly new shop.

To say this is not to be faithless, though it is to lay oneself open to that charge. When I was a minister in the 1970s, in a huge Glasgow housing scheme, less than one per cent of the population attended any of the Protestant churches. Some, outside the situation, suggested that this might be because the established church did not preach the gospel! When it was pointed out that the tiniest congregations were those of the biblically conservative groups, the rejoinder was that God did not promise popularity! This kind of circularity born of desperation does not wash. Those living and/or working in the situation, whether evangelical, liberal, radical or catholic, tended to a more realistic view. The traditional game is up; indeed it was up a long time ago. There is no point in applying rouge to the face of the corpse.

Admitting the death might permit new thoughts of resurrection; but please, please not too quickly or cheaply. The poor are not a 'problem' to which the church offers 'solutions' any more than the Resurrection is the 'solution' to the 'problem' of the Cross. The experience of negation is not swallowed up by the experience of affirmation.

Indeed, the problem/solution mentality, with all its technocratic and manipulative undergirding, distorts this matter. What we need to look for is not solutions but new directions, tentative ways of moving towards more reality, more light, more faithfulness.

For those who have ears to hear and eyes to see, there are modern-day hints and signs, and parables of the Kingdom among the poor. (This should hardly surprise readers of the New Testament.) The Kingdom of God is somewhat elusive (now you see it, now you don't), but there are glimpses, glimpses. These signs are not always 'religious'. They are often very, very earthy, to do with politics and neighbourliness and housing. There are many flowers in the concrete jungle.

What of the church? The churches are, of course, both part of the solution and part of the problem. This is because they are rooted in the community even though they be tiny minorities and they are not just colonies of heaven, but outposts of a well-meaning but anxious Scottish ecclesiastical empire whose theological and economic point of gravity lies somewhere on the Edinburgh–Dunblane axis.

Can it be that the tiny and vulnerable Christian communities at the end of the Protestant line will stammeringly teach the wider church how to live in the twenty-first century?

This book names realities and explores issues to which the church would rather, to use the Glasgow parlance, 'give the bodyswerve'.

John Harvey's ministries, in decaying Gorbals, cosmopolitan Iona, housing-scheme Raploch and inner-city Govan, have equipped him to be our guide. He is one of that rare breed — a Christian radical who loves the church. This book should be required reading for the Kirk.

Ron Ferguson
Leader, Iona Community

I

A look into the gap

Definitions

I have lived and worked over these past two decades mainly in areas of multiple deprivation in Scotland, in Glasgow and in Stirling, and my chief interest has been, and still is, in the formation of the church amongst the poor. Clearly both these terms — 'the church' and 'the poor' — require further definition; I shall try to explore their meaning in more detail in succeeding chapters, and their reality will continue to challenge us all along. I must begin, however, at the place at which all theological reflection on the church in the world always begins: the place where I am. For as it was with Moses so it is with us; the 'holy ground' is the place where we are standing, in the midst of our daily work, and it is there that God seeks to reveal Himself to us as the Living and present One — the great 'I AM'.

My place, then, is in Govan, in Glasgow, in 1987, as a Church of Scotland minister within the parish and congregation of Govan Old. I can think of no better way to get into my subject than to offer you a fairly quick analysis of this place, both parish and congregation, as it heads towards the last decade of the twentieth century.

Parish profiles

Fortunately, for our purpose, the Kirk Session of Govan Old decided to do a detailed analysis of both parish and congregation only three years ago, over the winter of 1983-84. They called it a 'Parish Profile', and it was seen as the necessary prelude to decisions about the future direction of our missionary task in Govan, particularly as we approach the centenary of our present church building in 1988. Centenaries, of course, are mainly useful as pegs to hang things on — or perhaps better, — 'springboards to jump forward from'; and while we in Govan Old have much to look back on with pride and pleasure, all the way to our foundation

11

by St Constantine in the sixth century, it is the future which is our main concern, both in thinking about the forthcoming centenary, and in undertaking our Parish Profile.

Let me tell you, first of all, how we came to decide to do this Parish Profile. We held an Elders' Conference in the spring of 1983 — an annual event which, that year, because we were too late to book up anywhere else, we held in the Pearce Institute, a huge Edwardian building next to the Parish Church, and closely associated with its work. At that conference — it lasted only for an afternoon and evening — we talked together about our church, and what we should be doing in Govan. It was a salutary, if also a fairly painful, discussion. We saw that we were, on the whole, a fairly elderly, pretty small, if nevertheless quite active and lively bunch of people who mainly lived and worked outwith the parish. We spoke of our worship — perhaps unique in its liturgy in the Church of Scotland — to us a liturgy of great meaning and value, to some a strange and foreign affair. We talked about our activities as a congregation — traditional in just about every way, with a Woman's Guild and Sunday Schools, uniformed organisations and youth groups — the sort of organisations you would expect to find in any congregation in the country. We came on to wonder how we could make contact with the hundreds, if not thousands, around our doors who were, as we put it, 'outside the church'?

Interest groups
Here we stumbled and fell. We looked back. What about starting up a Young Women's Group?, said someone. We looked at each other. Who, in Govan, would come? What about a Men's Association, we asked? We looked around and asked the same draughty question — who would come? Do we need to start up a Youth Club we wondered — but there were already a number of Youth Clubs in the parish, including right there in the Pearce Institute. Our discussion bumped along, interspersed with periods of silence that grew longer and longer — periods in which we looked with increasing confusion at the wall charts we had pinned to the walls of our conference room earlier, full of biblical quotations and exhortations on 'being the Church in the world', 'doing mission', and so on and so forth. Then, slowly, people began to say things which held seeds of liberation and hope. We began to talk about the people of our parish. Elders with a closer knowledge of the parish spoke up. A teacher spoke of what she knew: of broken

families, of single parents, of delinquency and courage and drug abuse and the struggle for survival. A shipyard worker spoke of what he knew: of uncertainty and unemployment and the pressure on families in the parish as the recession deepened in Clydeside. Another elder spoke of what he knew: of local action groups struggling for improvements in the areas of housing, of welfare, of relations with the police. The conversation warmed up; a growing sense of reality took over; and then we came to the question we knew was still waiting to be asked: 'so what do we do now?' The answer we found ourselves giving led to the decision to do the Parish Profile; for we had glimpsed, not only something of the nature of our parish, but much more of the depth of our own ignorance of it. We needed to find out what really was the face — or perhaps even the farce — of our parish before we could go one step further on.

There are many ways of doing a Parish Profile, or whatever you may call it; Dr John Vincent's Urban Theology Unit in Sheffield offers perhaps the most systematic method available in Britain today, and of course examples from the churches in the United States abound. We however simply did our own thing: we set up, in typical Presbyterian fashion, an *ad hoc* committee of three and told them to get on with it. With hindsight, I would not advise that as the best way; many more people should have been involved, and we should have taken the chance to start a much wider discussion amongst the congregation than we in fact did. But hindsight, of course, is a marvellous thing; at the time we thought we were being pretty adventurous; and the result, when we gathered a year later to look at it, was certainly revealing.

The statistics
What did we find? We found, first of all, a parish of about 4500 people set in a wider urban area of multiple deprivation — Greater Govan — containing about 22 000 souls. Our people, we found, lived in houses mainly owned and managed by community-based housing associations, with church members quite heavily involved in the management committee of one of them. These homes were mainly rehabilitated tenement property dating back to the first part of this century or the latter part of the last; and while many were in very good shape indeed, others were inadequate in a number of respects. In Greater Govan, of which we were a part, just over half the population fell into the 18–64 age group, and just

under a quarter were over 65; we had a higher proportion of single-parent families in our midst compared to the average for Glasgow as a whole. As to employment, we boasted, if that is the correct term, at that time 37 per cent adult unemployment and 62 per cent youth unemployment — the figures have since considerably increased. The majority of the population fell into the 'low income group' category; and the Regional Council's own Area Profile for Greater Govan identified, among our main problems, such issues as: the elderly, single parents, the unemployed, drug abuse, young people, and above all, problems arising from sheer lack of money.

In our area we noted the existence of many of the usual groups and institutions: schools, youth clubs, community halls, action groups, political parties, pubs, bingo halls, snooker clubs, small shops, larger chain-stores, and here and there the odd commercial activity; there was, just and no more, our shipyard, although its workforce came mainly from outwith the area. But in many of these we saw that the activists were a tiny minority and often the same people, wearing any number of hats and growing more and more tired by the year; we noted that the cinema had just closed, that one of the two bingo halls was closing, that people were, as it were, retreating in the face of the problems of the place, taking refuge in their homes — and often, particularly in the case of the children, getting out of the place at weekends, for example to their grannies or aunties in Pollok or Priesthill.

So if it was showing itself to us as an area in which the depopulation and demolition of the 1970s had 'bottomed out', Govan was also showing itself to us as an area of depression and retreat in many ways. Not that everyone was down and out; for what we also saw was that, even in the midst of these difficulties, many people were living very positive, and even upbeat, sorts of lives. But of one thing we became very quickly and very powerfully aware; they were not, by and large, living them in the church.

About one-tenth of the population of our ecclesiastical parish, we estimated, had any official church connection. Our own congregation, of course, provided us with the most accurate — and the most revealing — statistics. Our communion roll then stood at just over 500 people. Of these, about 12 per cent lived within our parish boundaries. By far the largest number — just over 60 per cent — lived in a wide circle around the parish area, mostly having been rehoused in the sixties and seventies, and having kept their church connection when they moved. Our membership was far and away female in composition — 75 per cent — and predominantly over 50 in age-grouping. The only other major church group in our parish was the Roman Catholic church of St Anthony's; it numbered just on 500 also, although, as is normally the case with Roman Catholic churches, its membership lived almost entirely within the parish area. But it, too, was predominantly female, and mainly elderly; again, like so many Roman Catholic churches, many more of the members actually attended worship than was the case in our own congregation where our average attendance at the main service of worship on a Sunday morning was about 150.

A Parish Church?

To put it bluntly, what we discovered about ourselves was that we were a parish church in little except name. Our membership was not of the parish; it did not reflect the make-up of the parish; and its interests on weekdays, unless in relation to the running of specific church organisations, were outwith the parish. There could be no denying the, at times sacrificial, service and commitment to the worship, the fabric and the activities of the church by a minority of activists, — and we estimated about 25 per cent of our women members and about 20 per cent of our men were in this category. But at the same time we estimated that only about 10–12 per cent of our entire membership were actively involved in the concerns of the parish outwith the church — and it should be noted that this 10 per cent was not the same 10 per cent who lived in the parish, although there was an overlap.

The gulf between church and parish becomes even plainer when we look at the position of those from the parish who wanted to 'join the church', or who came to seek baptism for their children. Since 1981, we have had on average two New Communicants' classes per year, each running for about three months, and the average number of people who stayed the course in each class was five. Of these, a minority were people with no previous church connection who lived within the parish, and these were mainly women, whose main reason for wanting to join the church was because they initially came seeking baptism for their children. The Church of Scotland, in common with other denominations is, at least officially, fairly strict about baptism of infants, insisting that, in the main, at least one of the parents should be a member of the

Church, either already or in the process of so becoming, before an infant is baptised. Quite properly, the Church seeks to present the Sacrament of baptism in the context of the on-going life of the Christian person and the Christian community — a start to the life of grace, rather than a one-off event of a mainly social character. The social and family pressures to 'get the baby christened', however, are still fairly strong in areas such as ours; and when it is put to parents that there is more to it than simply turning up on the Sunday morning, very often they are quite happy to join a New Communicants' class, and eventually to become communicant members of the church by profession of faith, without in the least feeling that they have been blackmailed.

But the fact has also to be faced that, in the majority of cases, their active connection with the Church gradually diminishes after the baptism of their children. They remain on the roll; they attend worship from time to time; they occasionally take part in other church activities; and sometimes their children come to Sunday School when they grow older. But the evidence cannot be avoided; their membership of the church is not normally a major life-changing and life-involving event, no matter how solemn the vows that they obediently repeat at their service of admission, and take on behalf of their babies at the sacrament of baptism. So congregations agonise over the trickle of New Communicants who trickle in and trickle out; and the minister, who is usually responsible for their preparation for admission, as he is for the preparation for baptism, wonders and worries about his failure to make it stick.

The situation I have been describing, with the aid of the Parish Profile from one inner-city congregation is, of course, incomplete and partial. It highlights weaknesses rather than strengths; and if one thing is sure, it is the sheer strength of survival of the institutional church in such areas, often in spite of, rather than because of, the attitude of the parent body of the wider church. Nevertheless, the situation I have been describing, however partial, is a common one, to be found not just in the inner areas of our cities, but also in the large housing schemes on the peripheries of our urban areas. When we turn, therefore, to ask why the situation is as it is, it is with some surprise that we have to recognise that very few attempts have been made to struggle with this situation in a disciplined and objective way and such attempts that have been made do not seem to have made any great difference to the strategy of the church at large as it seeks to plant itself amongst the poor in Scotland today.

Let me try to be more specific. There has been an almost total failure, within the Church of Scotland at least, to undertake a consistent, demanding and detailed analysis of the reasons why the poor are not anywhere near the church today. This failure viewed in the light of the church's clear purpose and immense resources, is not only surprising; it is disobedient, it is potentially and in many cases actually, disastrous, and it points to what I shall argue is a heretical view of what the church actually is, in the current thinking of the Church of Scotland.

Reports to the General Assembly

For the moment, let us confine ourselves to an attempt to clarify the actual situation, to discover some of the principal reasons for the absence of the poor from the church. From the 'official' church, there have appeared one or two markers — tentative, and largely ignored. In 1969, the General Assembly set up, under the convenership of Professor Hugh Anderson, a Special Commission on Priorities of Mission in Scotland in the 1970s.[1] In its report in 1971, this Commission identified four main areas in which the church was 'out of touch' with the world. It saw the church as 'part of the middle-class sub-culture', and thus remaining 'alien to many people's lives'. It saw the local congregation as being an 'ineffective community', resulting in 'a lack of expectancy that the church has anything of value to say about the life of the world'. It saw the church as seeming 'to belong only to the domestic/leisure/relaxation sector of man's relationships, while many of the decisions which determine social structures and affect the quality of life are·made elsewhere'. It criticised the very parochialness of the church, resulting in 'congregations tending to be isolated from each other, and seeing their loyalty within too limited a horizon'.

These are all valid points, and we shall return to them later. The Church of Scotland, however, moved on from them with hardly a murmur to appoint another Special Commission, this time with a much grander remit: 'to interpret for the Church the purpose towards which God is calling His people in Scotland, to investigate and assess the resources of the Church in persons and property, and to make recommendations for the reshaping of the life and structure of the Church'. This remit the Committee of Forty, as it came to be called, struggled to fulfil — and produced much useful material in the process. Its analysis, however, was too wide — which is not perhaps surprising, in view of the vast scale of its remit — and, at least in the popular version of its findings, entitled *People with a Purpose*[2], no analysis of the gap between the church and the poor finds a place. The result of all this, again at the level of the 'official' church thinking on the matter, is that, to quote the Secretary of the Church's Department of Ministry and Mission[3], 'we have no one policy of Urban Mission unless it be to support as much as we can those in the parishes', although he adds, 'I would certainly agree that Urban Mission is vastly important for the whole pattern of the Church in Scotland.' Colin Day, the former Field Secretary of the 'Tell Scotland' Movement of the 1950s and early 1960s, is more specific[4]: 'The Institutional church seemed and seems unable to let go its ecclesiastical structures and identity; it speaks of re-formation but really means rehabilitation, doing the old thing better, not new things different-ly. There is still teaching by telling, with little emphasis on learning by discovery together, little dialogue and a dependence on authority by statement rather than by agreement.'

Clearly, if we wish to understand why there is this huge gap between the church and the poor, we must therefore look else-where than the 'official' church for some help. In the 1960s, the World Council of Churches' (WCC) Department on Studies In Evangelism undertook a long and detailed examination of *The Missionary Structure of the Congregation*[5]. Among the many valuable insights that it amassed from the world church in this study, comes this from Professor Hans Margull of Hamburg University[6]: 'Structural fundamentalism seems to involve a wides-pread but dormant "view" in which structural problems involving church and congregation are not held to be decisive questions for the church . . . it is present innocently in situations where the historicity of faith and of Christian existence is otherwise recog-nised and accepted.' In other words, here we have an authoritative indication of one of the main causes for the gap — the refusal of the church to recognise that its own structures are a large part of the problem, meaning by 'structures' not so much its own structures of bureaucracy and administration (which seem to have been the structural problem as identified by the Assembly Council of the Church of Scotland which was set up following the final report of the Committee of Forty), but rather the structures of the church at the local level of church life and witness. It is here, at the grassroots, that Dr Margull sees the real problem arising. He identifies it as 'parish paralysis', with a concentration on Christians 'coming' together for nourishment, with little or no appreciation of the corresponding command to 'go' into all the world; so that 'the very intimacy of the parish system emerges as the primary problem.' Both the Anderson Commission and the Committee of Forty, to be fair, pointed also to this problem, and recommended changes in local structures, both in terms of the creation of larger, and smaller, local groupings within the local Christian community. The Secretary of the Department of Ministry and Mission[7], however, does not see 'much response' to these recommendations 'in terms of formal structure (he notes the odd examples of house groups and Festivals of Faith as possible straws in the wind), and as to the whole of the WCC's thinking on mission as reflected in the Study on the Missionary Structure of the Congregation, he does not think it 'made much impact' — a conclusion with which one is forced to agree.

To imagine, however, that the gap would be closed if local congregations both united in larger groupings and broke down into smaller, more intimate ones, would be to ignore problems much deeper and more fundamental even than 'structural fundamentalism'. To attempt to identify what these are, we have to turn to individuals — and there are very few of them in print — who have struggled with the existence of this gap in their own local situations and experience. One of the influential books on this whole question, which came out in English in the late 1940s, was Abbé Michonneau's book *Revolution in a City Parish*[8]. Writing from the French urban situation of the war and the post-war period, he gives a fascinating and brutally honest insight into the real situation of the church in urban European Society. Among the most important of these insights are the following, highly relevant to our purpose:

— first, he identifies the importance to the poor of 'the group'[9]:

'The great majority of people are not aware of any personal capacities for individual thought; they are submerged in the vague "personality" of the group to which they belong . . . hence, it is impossible to draw them to Christ as individuals . . . the conquest must be a collective one.'

This is overstated, in my view, and based still on what is largely an outsider's view of the poor, but it is nevertheless extremely important, for Michonneau is entirely correct in pointing to the importance to the poor of what we would now call class solidarity, a phrase which has been overlaid with highly political implications, but which nonetheless points to an inherent reality in the life of the poor which the Church ignores to its shame and to its peril. It is a factor to which we shall return in a later chapter in some detail.

— second, Michonneau criticises the church's dependence on what he calls 'parish activities'. These, he claims,[10] 'have grown to be obstacles, and not aids, to the apostolate,' as the church

'everlastingly tries to organise life and society as though we were in a majority! The fact is that we are a very small minority. Our attempts to set in motion all sorts of Christian activities are really nothing but superficial efforts. We may as well admit that we are in a pagan world.'

Again this is overstated and one wants to speak a little in defence of some of the excellent work done by many of these parish activities of which we all have experience — the Guild, the Bible class, the Church youth group, the uniformed organisations, and so on. Nevertheless, we ignore Michonneau's criticism at our peril, for, as we shall see when we come to consider the experience of someone much nearer home, the danger of our over-concentration on the activities and successes of these parish activities is that we find ourselves creating a 'church' world for our parishioners, as distinct from the 'real' world they live in day by day — and a 'church' world, moreover, which is marked by very definite cultural and secular characteristics quite alien to the poor.

— third, Michonneau points to the internal pressure operating within the church which leads to the creation and maintenance of middle-class values, a point picked up as of primary importance by the Anderson Commission in 1971. 'Everything about our training' claims Michonneau[11], 'seems pointed to a final product which will be polished to a bright middle-class lustre. In the face of this, we express surprise when our graduates are unwilling to go back to their native working class. We have made this practically impossible.' As we shall see later, this criticism is highly relevant in Scotland today; in particular the church's emphasis on middle-class values, and its constant condemnation of working class values, has eroded its credibility amongst the poor in our country and yet we have scarcely noticed it.

In the 1950s, Tom Allan's little book entitled *The Face of My Parish*[12], attempted both to document his powerful evangelistic experiment with his North Kelvinside congregation in mission work in his parish, and to assess the results and the problems it threw up. I am not concerned here with the details of the experiment, which I intend to examine in a later chapter; but it is relevant at this point to look at some of his conclusions. In many respects they follow Michonneau, to whom Allan acknowledged his deep personal indebtedness at the start of his book:

— first, reflecting on the problem of what he calls the 'assimilation' into the church of new members from his mission (an impressive 800 in five and a half years' work), he points to what he calls 'the secularism of the church'. 'Parishioners joining the church', he says[13] 'felt themselves alienated from their own class', and found themselves forced into 'a culture pattern which separates the church from the mass of the people'. With Michonneau, Allan has seen that the gap is not just to be measured in distance of care and structure; it is to be measured also in terms of class and culture; indeed, and here we move quite a large step forward in our understanding of the nature of the gap between the poor and the church, it is necessary, claims Allan[14], to recognise that the church has 'reduced the offence of the Cross to a doctrine' and 'has transformed the revolutionary ethic of Jesus into an inoffensive prudential morality'. Of this 'revolutionary ethic of Jesus' we shall have much more to say.

— the second very valuable point Allan makes is a necessary corrective to the all-too-common response of the Church of Scotland to the problems of mission in the modern world. He quotes with approval the words of Daniel Jenkins[15]:

'What we must deliver ourselves from is the notion expressed by many enthusiastic spirits in these days, that the gospel is not triumphantly spread abroad because we fail to "sell" it effectively enough, and that all we need is to be more energetic, dynamic, up-to-date and super-efficient.'

In other words, beware, says Allan, of the temptation to solve the problem by bringing in the 'popular preacher' and 'church growth' experts; wise words, however puzzling they may seem to us as coming from the man who went on, very shortly after they were quoted with such obvious approval, to organise the 'All-Scotland Crusade' and to bring the American popular evangelist,

Billy Graham, to the country. Reading them, one is reminded of the somewhat cynical words of Michonneau on preaching[16]:

'If we wish to make a show of our great knowledge, the congregation cannot prevent us; neither can they assimilate what we are trying to say. When we soar, we soar alone', and without, one must add, the majority of our parishioners even being there to hear us — for they are not in the pews on a Sunday morning anyway.

Finally, for the moment, we turn to a sociologist, Peter Sissons, who in 1973, on behalf of the Church of Scotland, produced a detailed analysis of church membership in the burgh of Falkirk in central Scotland[17]. Sissons points, in the first place, to the failure of the church to think through 'the levels of meaning associated with "being religious" and belonging to a religious group'. He adds[18]:

'There is sometimes a tacit assumption that church planning is concerned exclusively with behaviour to the neglect of the total religious comprehension of the church member or potential church member and of his world view'.

And what he means by this is spelled out very clearly a little further on[19]:

'There prevails amongst the members of the Church of Scotland a broad approval of the Calvinist emphasis upon thrift and dedication to work which is extended into a general assumption that ambition and aspiration to worldly achievement are evidence of a right attitude to the world .... Those with no ambitions or no occupational aspirations would hardly be likely to find the social worlds of the churches to be conducive; particularly is this the case with regard to the Church of Scotland with its large proportion of male church members with fulfilled ambitions.'

And again[20]:

'The non-aspiring manual worker and his family would find little to attract them to the social world which is embodied by the Church of Scotland ... many of them were sympathetic towards the churches but felt they belonged to a different social world from that inhabited by the church members'.

And[21]:

'It is the social world constituted by church membership which provides the greatest stumbling block for the non church members, not the church as an ideal institution or belief in religion . . . religion is something you take part in, rather than something you believe.'

His findings conclusively showed[22] that:

'the majority of non-church members did not identify with the church to a large extent because they had been unable to identify themselves as "church people". The world of the church and of religion constituted an alien world for them.'

In other words, and here I draw on my own experience of having heard this said to me many times over twenty years, 'the church is no for the likes of us'. How true!

The gap

In this opening chapter, I have sought only to describe the gap that exists between the church and the poor in urban Scotland today, and to point, in a preliminary way, to what I believe are some of the reasons for its existence. That there *is* a gap is not in any serious doubt — and this can be affirmed even before we have examined in more detail both the nature of the church and of the poor. But if further evidence is needed than what I have adduced so far from one inner city parish, then it can be found. Unfortunately, it cannot be found in one publication where it might have been expected, the booklet entitled *Prospects for Scotland*[23], setting out the findings and analysis of a Census of Church attendance in 1984. Here again, the interest seems more on the wider trends and the grander hopes, with some attention paid to the breakdown of church attendance in terms of denomination, geography, age and sex, but sadly, no attempt made to look at the situation in terms of class or economic grouping. But there are other sources, such as local surveys; one was done in Easterhouse, a housing scheme of some 40 000 people in Glasgow, in the early 1970s, which showed that of those who called themselves 'Protestant' there, one per cent had a live church connection, while of those who called themselves 'Catholic', five per cent were active in their church attendance. A report to Glasgow Presbytery[24] on the situation of the churches in what it called the 'Inner Ring' of the city, made in the early 1960s, shows clearly that 'the vast majority within the Inner Ring areas are totally outside the life of the Church'. An examination of the make-up of the Church of Scotland's Committees — from Kirk Sessions through Presbyteries to the General Assembly, will readily reveal the absence, in the national church, at the representative level, of a very large section of the population — namely, the poor. Or compare the economic and numerical situations of congregations in areas of multiple deprivation with congregations in areas of relative affluence; the gap stands revealed in abundant detail.

Why is it there? It is not simply because of the unfaithfulness of the Christian people in poor areas, because of the failure of the ministers of the church, or because we somehow cannot 'sell' the faith well enough to the poor; to seek an answer along any of these lines would be to play with fire, would be to turn 'faith' into a 'work' to be marketed in a competitive world. The evidence indicates, I believe, that to seek to understand the gap, we have to look more in the areas of structural fundamentalism, of what Sissons calls 'the embourgoisement activity' of the church, of the insistent and pernicious separation of the world of the church from the world of the poor, of the alienation that accompanies any form of conversion from one to the other, and of the very nature of the life of the poor itself. To this, but first to the very nature of the church itself, we must now turn in the next two chapters.

References
1 Church of Scotland (1971).
2 Church of Scotland (1978).
3 In a private letter to the author.
4 In a private letter to the author.
5 World Council of Churches (1967).
6 World Council of Churches (1967), p19; see also Williams (1963), p12ff.
7 In a private letter to the author.
8 Michonneau (1949).
9 Michonneau (1949), p7.
10 Michonneau (1949), p54ff.
11 Michonneau (1949), p131ff.
12 Allan (1954).
13 Allan (1954), p39ff.
14 Allan (1954), p42
15 Allan (1954), p14.
16 Michonneau (1949), p134.
17 Sissons (1973).
18 Sissons (1973), p276f.
19 Sissons (1973), p290.
20 Sissons (1973), p290.

21 Sissons (1973), p257.
22 Sissons (1973), p265f.
23 Brierley and Macdonald (1985).
24 Report on 'The Inner ring' made to Glasgow Presbytery (c.1960).

II

The Church and its purpose

Religious roots

A group of American college students, led by their college
chaplain, set off in the early 1970s for a three-month tour of
European religious communities. Their stated purpose was to try
to find their religious roots; disillusioned with years of campaign-
ing for this and that cause without much success, they had
increasingly felt the need to know the basis on which they were
trying to stand. After spending time at Protestant, Roman Catholic and Anglican communities on the Continent and in England,
they ended up for their last visit at the Iona Community in
Scotland. There, to their great disappointment, they found no
monks; no strict religious life; no Benedictine offices; and a large
number of people about their own age who conducted the services,
argued late into the night about many issues, and ran the place in
an open, often chaotic, fashion. In the middle of their two-week
stay, things came to a head. The Community's staff, fed up with
the young Americans' obvious disapproval and their idealistic
notions of what the church and life should be like, demanded a
show-down. For two hours, in the ancient chapter-house of the
medieval Abbey, the accusations and counter-accusations flew, in
a way which would have made the old Iona monks turn in their
graves. But at the end of that remarkable meeting, much air had
been cleared; and during the second week of their stay, the
American and British young people were able to talk much more
realistically with each other — particularly about the issue which
was obviously now at the top of the Americans' minds — how do
we fit in now to the church when we get back home?

I remember the event vividly, and it will serve to introduce the
subject of this chapter: what is the church, and what is the church
for? The two questions, it seems to me, must always go together. It
may be a constant temptation to imagine that we can find an ideal
church — and the young American college students were not

alone in their search. Nor is it enough to speak about the church as being both a divine and a human activity, if by saying that we are then led into the temptation to regard the divine part as fixed and final, and the human part as temporary and sinful and at risk. There can be, in my view, no speaking of the church without immediately being involved in a variety of tensions; the tension between the church and its purpose, the tension between the church and its past, the tension between the church and the world, to name but three. It is in the midst of these tensions that the people who are the church have to live; where the people who respond in faith to the Risen Christ and His message about the Kingdom of God interact with the world, past, present and future, still on pilgrimage, yet in the power of the Spirit.

Liberation theology
In much of what I say about the church and its purpose, it will be obvious that I am indebted to recent work done by some Latin American theologians of what is called the Liberation Theology school. I should make it clear at the outset, however, that while I go to them, and gratefully, for help, we should not look to them for all the answers. Nor would they expect us to, for their essential message is that to understand what God is doing today in the church and in the world, we have to get up off our knees in the place where we are, and be obedient in action once again. They cannot do that for us — we must do that for ourselves.

I raise first a matter which may sound rather academic, but which I believe is of first importance in approaching this subject. I described the church above as 'the people who respond in faith to the Risen Christ and His message about the Kingdom of God'. This raises the question: where is the focus of faith to be for the church? In much of the teaching of the church today, as in the past, it is Christ, and Christ alone, who is presented as this focus. This focus on Christ is to be found, of course, also in the historic creeds and confessions of the church. Now there can be no questioning the centrality of the person of Christ to the Christian faith; and when I confess my faith every week in the words of the Apostles' Creed, the phrases about belief in Christ build up my faith in many ways. However, there is a very real danger here which is this: by making Christ, and Christ alone the sole focus of faith, we run the danger of christological reduction. Professor Jon Sobrino of San Salvador puts it this way[1]:

'This could lead to locating the response to the gospel message more in the line of faith and personal contact with Christ than in the line of the accomplishment of God's Kingdom. The demands of Christian practice would certainly be regarded as important, but they would be regarded as secondary to and deducible from the first and fundamental response, namely, faith in Christ and contact with him. This would lead in turn to a one-sided relation with Christ and a devalution of the Kingdom of God'.

Just as there can be no talk of the church without talk also of what the church is for, so there can be no talk about Christ without talk also about the Kingdom of God. The faith of the church is faith in the Risen Christ and His message about the Kingdom of God. The Gospels make this abundantly clear, with their firm presentation of the opening proclamation of Jesus: 'The right time has come, and the Kingdom of God is near! Turn away from your sins and believe the Good News!' (Mark 1:14 and also Matt. 4:17 and Luke 4:16–21.) Much has been written about the centrality of the Kingdom of God for Jesus, and it need not be rehearsed here.

The Kingdom of God

Before moving on to look at the nature of this divine Kingdom, let us recall the Lord's Prayer. The central petition here, in the version of Matthew 6:9–13, is 'may your Kingdom come'. This is widely agreed — but what may not be so generally noticed is that the whole of the rest of the prayer hangs, as it were, from that cry for the coming of God's Kingdom. In the Kingdom, God's will *will* be done, on earth as in heaven — for what is any Kingdom but the place where the king's will is done? In the Kingdom, there will be food for all — the petition is to give *us*, not *me*, daily bread, or bread enough for today, and we can therefore never rest content until we *all* have it, not just ourselves alone. Central to the very life of the Kingdom, has to be a life of forgiveness — so we are told to pray for it, and to pray also for the grace to forgive others. Finally, in the Kingdom, there will be no need for us to test God, which I take to be the meaning of the phrase 'do not bring us to hard testing' — for in the Kingdom, the proper relationship between the Creator and His creatures will have been restored; the apple, as it were, will be back on the tree.

The focus of the faith of the church, then, is the Risen Christ and His message about the Kingdom of God, which is amazing when you look at what happened to the historical Jesus and His message about the Kingdom of God. The powerful people of His day, and especially the leaders of religion in Israel, violently rejected both Him and His message, but the poor, the people on the 'underside of history', to use Gutierrez's[2] colourful phrase, received both Him and His message with gladness, amounting at times to wild enthusiasm. To understand both the nature of the church and the purpose of the church, then, we must look in more detail at why there were these two very different responses to Jesus and His message about the Kingdom — we must look back, in other words, to try to see how Jesus, and His message, clicked, or failed to click, with the people who heard Him.

Central to the faith of Israel, as found in the Old Testament, is both the reality and the promise of the Kingdom of God. It is there, of course, in the Creation stories, in both versions: in the Priestly version, presenting a view of the whole world (not simply the Jewish part of it) ordered by God in justice and in plenty, with its recurring refrain, 'and God was pleased with what He saw'; and in the Yahwist's version, where everything is seen as in a right relationship with both itself and with Yahweh who made it. In both Leviticus and in Deuteronomy, we find many examples of the importance attached by the law-givers of Israel to the mainte-nance of that Kingdom of God, in justice and in plenty, amongst the people of God. Especially in chapter 19 of Leviticus, we are given laws for Holiness and Justice; the leaving of uncut corn and fallen grapes for the poor after the harvest (v.9); the call to honesty and justice in the law courts (v.15); the call to love neighbour as self (v.18); the exhortation to care for and respect the elderly (v.32); and above all the laws concerning the Year of Jubilee, or Restoration in chapter 25, verses 8–55, ending with the ringing statement: 'An Israelite cannot be a permanent slave, because the people of Israel are the Lord's slaves. He brought them out of Egypt; He is the Lord their God'. In the book of Deuteronomy, the people of Israel are warned time and again that all will only go well with them if they remember the centrality of the Kingdom of God — a warning perhaps encapsulated best in chapter 16, verse 20: 'Always be fair and just, so that you will occupy the land that the Lord your God is giving you and will continue to live there for ever'.

The eighth century B.C. prophets, Isaiah, Amos, Micah and Zephaniah, are at pains to warn against what they see as all kinds of oppression and crimes against the Kingdom of God, arising out of the situation of economic growth and prosperity which applied in Israel in their time. Isaiah calls to them to 'see that justice is done — help those who are oppressed, give orphans their rights, and defend widows' (1:17); he pronounces doom on the rich women of Jerusalem (3:16-24) and on those who unscrupulously gather wealth to themselves (5:8-16), and he hammers those who pervert religion by committing gross injustice while undertaking religious exercises in the famous chapter 58 on the nature of true fasting. In chapter 61, in a lyrical passage quoted at the start of His ministry by Jesus, Isaiah directly relates his message to the laws concerning the Year of Jubilee in Leviticus:

'The Sovereign Lord has filled me with His spirit. He has chosen me and sent me to bring good news to the poor, to heal the brokenhearted, to announce release to the captives and freedom to those in prison. He has sent me to proclaim that the time has come when the Lord will save His people and defeat their enemies'. (vs.1-2).

In Amos, the same notes are sounded with, if anything, a sharper edge:

'The Lord says, "The people of Israel have sinned again and again, and for this I will certainly punish them. They sell into slavery honest men who cannot pay their debts, poor men who cannot even repay the price of a pair of sandals. They trample down the weak and helpless, and push the poor out of the way"'. (2:6-7)

The result of all this oppression, as Amos sees it, is God's rejection of the whole religious cult of Israel, in favour of the imperative return to the life of the Kingdom:

'I hate your religious festivals; I cannot stand them. When you bring me burnt offerings, and grain offerings, I will not accept them; I will not accept the animals you have fattened to bring me as offerings. Stop your noisy songs; I do not want to listen to your harps. Instead, let justice flow like a stream, and righteousness like a river that never goes dry'. (5:21-24).

Isaiah, especially in chapters 9 and 11, introduces a new note concerning the Kingdom of God when he speaks of the coming of the future King who will protect the poor and restore God's Kingdom. This King, cries the prophet, will 'rule as King David's successor, basing His power on right and justice, from now until the end of time'. (9:7) He 'will not judge by appearance or hearsay; He will judge the poor fairly, and defend the rights of the helpless'. (11:3–4)

Zephaniah, in chapter 2, verse 3, clearly identifies the source to which the poor and the oppressed must turn for help: 'Turn to the Lord, all you humble people of the land, who obey His commands. Do what is right, and humble yourselves before the Lord'.

In all this, there are certain important aspects of the nature of the Kingdom of God and of human involvement in it to be noted. Nowhere in these parts of the Old Testament is poverty either accepted as fate (kismet), or idealised; it is contrary to the will of God, and is to be struggled against with might and main. However, it is a struggle which is to be conducted entirely with reference to the will, and the promised involvement in the struggle, of the Lord God.

Before we leave the Old Testament, we should notice that the Psalms are often the means by which the poor of Yahweh express this hope and this struggle. Thus, in Psalm 40, verse 17: 'I am weak and poor, O Lord, but you have not forgotten me. You are my Saviour and my God — hurry to my aid!'; in Psalm 72, verses 12–14: 'He rescues the poor who call to Him, and those who are needy and neglected. He has pity on the weak and the poor; He saves the lives of those in need. He rescues them from oppression and violence; their lives are precious to Him'; and Psalm 109, verses 30–31: 'I will give loud thanks to the Lord; I will praise Him in the assembly of the people, because He defends the poor man, and saves him from those who condemn him to death'. There are many other examples.

In view of this central concern for the Kingdom of God as a God-given time of justice and plenty, with special protection for the poor, and an end to their suffering and oppression, it is hardly surprising that, when Jesus came announcing the imminent arrival of this Kingdom in His own person, and then proceeded to act as if in fact it already had arrived, the poor heard Him gladly, and welcomed Him ecstatically when He rode into Jerusalem on Palm Sunday. There undoubtedly were some in that crowd who were shouting and cheering because they thought He was coming as a political saviour, worried though they must have been to see Him riding a donkey rather than a war-horse; but for the majority on that fateful day, what they were cheering for was what their basic Jewish faith had taught them to hope for from the start; the coming of the Kingdom of God, with its justice and its plenty and its true freedom for the poor, for themselves. They knew themselves as blessed indeed, not because they were poor, but because the coming of the Kingdom of God in Jesus, in the words of Gutierrez[3] was going to 'put an end to their poverty by creating a world of brotherhood'.

In the New Testament, we first of all see Jesus, in the Gospels, taking up, as it were, where Isaiah left off, with his opening statement in Luke, as we have already mentioned, based on Isaiah's great passage in chapter 61 about the 'good news to the poor'. Jesus is then portrayed as going on to develop this message of the Kingdom of God in many ways. We see Him deepening it in the Beatitudes and in the Sermon on the Mount; of particular importance is Luke's version of the Beatitudes (6:20–22) where Jesus pronounces happiness on the poor, those who are hungry now, those who weep now, those who are hated, insulted, rejected, told they are evil wasters — 'the Kingdom of God is yours'. We see Him reinforcing it in the parables, time and again; we see Him stating it explicitly to His opponents. Thus, in Mark 2:17 'People who are well do not need a doctor, but only those who are sick. I have come not to call respectable people, but outcasts'. Or again, in Matthew 21:31–32 'I tell you, the tax collectors and prostitutes are going into the Kingdom of God ahead of you, for John the Baptist came to you showing you the right path to take, and you would not believe him, but the tax collectors and the prostitutes believed him. Even when you saw this, you did not later change your minds and believe him'. As we have already mentioned, Jesus backed up His words about the Kingdom of God and its essential nature, with His deeds; so that His opponents could not avoid seeing that He was a friend of tax collectors and outcasts, and sat down at table with the ritually unclean — even if they could not understand yet why He was doing it. Finally, the story of the Last Judgment, the Sheep and the Goats, is placed precisely by Matthew as the climax to Jesus' whole teaching and active ministry in chapter 25, where we are challenged unavoidably to see the face of Christ most clearly in the face of the poor. It is a statement fundamentally made to the church, and prompts the awesome judgment of José Miguez Bonino[4] 'The church which is not the church of the poor puts in serious jeopardy its churchly character'. To this we must return later.

In view of the tendency, especially of Protestant churchmanship, to see, in some way, the possession of worldly goods as being a mark of God's favour, we might, at this point, note the teaching of the New Testament on this. Quite simply, there is no New Testament authority for this view. Warnings against worldly riches abound in the letters. Thus James, in chapter 5, verses 1–6, gives a clear warning to the rich to 'weep and wail over the miseries that are coming upon you'; Paul, in his first letter to Timothy, advises him to 'command those who are rich in the things of this life not to be proud, but to place their hope, not in such an uncertain thing as riches, but in God, who generously gives us everything for our enjoyment'. The first letter of John is full of similar warnings, as in chapter 3, verse 17, where we read 'If a rich person sees his brother in need, yet closes his heart to his brother, how can he claim that he loves God?' In the Gospels, perhaps the clearest statement of Jesus' view of the proper use of worldly wealth is to be found in the story of the Prodigal Son, where, in Luke chapter 15, we read that the joyful father pours all sorts of marks of worldly riches, not on the honest, hardworking elder brother, but on the younger profligate rascal who has finally crawled back home.

Biblical evidence
Before we go on to look, quite briefly, at how the early church handled the message of the Kingdom of God, let us summarise the evidence of the Bible as it has been presented so far. What we have seen, is that the faith of the church is not simply in Christ alone, but in Christ and His message of the Kingdom of God. This message derives, as the people heard it and either received or rejected it, from the central message of the Jewish faith, as found especially in the Pentateuch, in the Prophets, and in the Psalms; and it is a message of a Kingdom of justice and plenty and right relationships, established by God, messed up and broken by men, and yet guaranteed by the will of God alone, and to be brought back in by Him. Basically, it is a message of hope for the poor and the oppressed, whose condition is not to be accepted as inevitable, but neither is it to be idealised; and when Jesus comes, proclaiming the imminent arrival of this same Kingdom by word and by action, the poor hear Him gladly, and He and His message are rejected violently by the respectable and the rich and the leaders of the religious establishment of His day. The New Testament church, however, gets the message, puts riches and worldly wealth

firmly in their place, recognises that the face of Christ is to be seen most clearly in the face of the poor, and even sets up a new community based on the message of the Kingdom, which they now see as being underwritten by God through His raising of Jesus from the dead — the new community of sharing, of caring and of economic equality as evidenced in Acts chapter 2, verses 43–47. They are living, with the Risen Christ, the life of the Kingdom of God now, these rag-tag-and-bobtail people, who from a human point of view, as Paul delights in reminding them in his first letter to the Corinthians, were neither 'wise nor powerful nor of high social standing' — the 'nonsense of the world', chosen 'to shame the wise', the 'weak of the world', chosen 'to shame the powerful', the 'despised, the no-users of the world', chosen to destroy 'what the world thinks is important'. Small wonder their contemporaries looked on in confusion and concern, and complained that they were 'turning the world upside down'.

It is not my intention here to attempt to follow the development of the church's handling of the message of the Kingdom of God down through the centuries. Others have written at length on this subject, and from a variety of viewpoints, and their opinions deserve more detailed attention. What is clear is that while the church, in the main, never lost its awareness of the whole world, and the struggle for a just social order, as the proper field of its obedience and its witness, this vision was rapidly compromised as the church grew in numbers and in influence, first in the collapsing world of the Roman Empire, and then in the confusing world of medieval Christendom, and eventually in the burgeoning world of capitalism, the industrial revolution, and scientific materialism. In all of these worlds, there is plenty of evidence to show that the church quite quickly came to mobilise its growing resources in a continuing attempt to help the poor and the oppressed, with varying degrees of success. It came to be a major provider of goods and services, both religious and material, *for* the poor; but it also, in the main, ceased to be a church *of* the poor, where the Kingdom of God as proclaimed by Jesus was both celebrated and struggled for, in the face of the hostility of the world.

There were, of course, voices raised in warning. The trilogy of books, published in the late 1970s by the World Council of Churches' Commission on the Churches' Participation in Development, under the editorship of Julio de Santa Ana, draw our attention to the words of two of the fathers of the Church which are relevant here. St Augustine, speaking of the desire for peace, says[5]: 'Do you think it is a great thing to desire peace? Any perverse man desires it. Well, it is a good thing, peace, but do justice, for justice and peace embrace each other and do right', and in saying so, echoes Psalm 85, verse 10: 'Justice and peace join hands'. The other quotation is from St John Chrysostom, speaking of the danger present when the church's accumulation of wealth began to discredit the church's gospel. 'This is why,' he cried[6], 'the Gentiles do not believe what we say. They want us to show them a doctrine not through our words but through our works. When they see us building magnificent houses, planting gardens, building baths, buying fields, however, they find it hard to believe that we are preparing a journey to another city'. Timeless words, these, and appropriate to almost any period in the history of the Christian church.

God's gift to the church
In this brief exploration into the nature of the church and its purpose, it is helpful to consider a pamphlet published by the Board of National Missions of the former United Presbyterian Church in the USA, sometime in the 1960s, entitled *The City — God's Gift to the Church*[7]. In this pamphlet the authors, whose names are not given, draw attention in Chapter 2 to the awareness of the New Testament writers, especially 1 Peter, that the embryonic church is in fact the new chosen people of God.

> 'You are the chosen race, the King's priests, the holy nation, God's own people, chosen to proclaim the wonderful acts of God, who called you out of darkness into His own marvellous light'.
> (1 Peter 2:9)

This is an exciting insight, carrying as it does with it the realisation that the church stands in succession to the ones with whom, from the very beginning, God made a special covenant in order that His Kingdom of justice and plenty and right relationships should be established in the whole world.

The church, in every century, and in every place, has made use of this description of itself, understandably; but the writers of this pamphlet point to an inherent danger in using it to which the church, particularly in the broken-down urban situations of today, is often quite blind, and which can be a very real cause of stumbling, especially to the poor:

'The city church is people — people of the city who have been called by Christ and belong to Him, but all too often the city church finds within the body members who have forgotten who it was who called them. In a word, they are the "self-chosen people". They look upon the church as their own property and seek to control its work in the light of their own aims and goals. They choose to make the church their own and no efforts of the "new minister" or "new elements" in the community can bring them to relinquish their grasp. In short, the city church finds within its doors, people who are at best withered hands and feet of Christ, because they have forgotten whose hands and feet they really are'.[8]

The authors of the pamphlet go on to examine the nature of the phenomenon of the self-chosen people from a sociological point of view, noting the inherent conservative tendency of such groups, and the urge to power and control felt and exercised by many who rise very quickly to positions of leadership within the often hard-pressed churches of our urban areas. For this reason, it might have seemed more appropriate to note this aspect of the nature of the gap between the church and the poor in our cities in the previous chapter. I have chosen to raise it here, however, in the context of our examination of what the church is and what it is for, because it seems to me to belong with our view of the nature of the church and its purpose, which is to be for others, in obedience to the mission of God in the world, and never to be for itself and its own understanding of mission.

The Anglican Archbishop William Temple may first have coined the phrase: 'The Church exists mainly for the sake of those outside it'. Not, let it quickly be said, in order to haul the outsiders inside — and in passing we may notice how much of the literature of mission, even yet, is filled with images of shepherds gathering sheep, fishermen netting fish, and swimmers saving drowning people by pulling them to the shore. Nevertheless, Temple's phrase is valuable, in so far as it points to the direction in which the church is called to move, which is always out, always seeking to share, always giving away, always 'losing its life in order to gain it', It moves in this direction, clearly, not because it has a pro-gramme of church growth, or because it is wise in the ways of the world, but rather because it is out in the world that it will find God; also the Risen Christ, who is already out in the world, before ever the church even arrives, bringing into being His Kingdom of justice and plenty and right relationships. The church's job is to go out to him outside the camp, to stand with him where he, and where the action, is, and there to open itself to Him and to His spirit, that the world may believe. Or, to use again the insight of Julio de Santa Ana, as he discusses the self-emptying, or *kenotic*, aspect of the nature of the church, in line with the self-emptying of the church's Lord as described in Philippians chapter 2:

> 'The people of God are a pilgrim people. They are a people on the move. They *have* to be. That movement has a sense, an orientation; it is movement towards love and justice. It is a movement which takes its dynamism from the hope in the King- dom of God'.[9]

Marks of the church

Finally, let us turn to the traditional 'marks of the church', as found in both Catholic and Protestant theology. The important thing for today's chuch is not to ensure that it fits in, that it relates to yesterday's definitions — we should be much more interested in tomorrow — but it would be discourteous, not to say unwise, to ignore the attempts of our fathers and mothers in the faith, as they struggled to set down the irreducible minimum for recognising the true church in the world.

The traditional Reformed position, in which I stand, gives the marks of the church as 'the Word truly preached, the Sacraments rightly administered, and discipline properly upheld'. These marks were identified at least in part in protest against the mess that the church had been making, for a long time, of the other marks of the church, to which we shall turn in a moment. They are, therefore, in some sense reactionary, which is understandable, but not always the best foundation for what are meant to be fundamental statements. Every so often, Reformed theologians seek to update them; to try to show that the Word is only truly preached if it is at the same time truly and obediently heard and acted upon, not only by those within the church, but also by those outside it, as indeed the Reformers themselves believed; to understand the right administration of the Sacraments, not just in terms of church order and discipline, but also of how they are done, where they are done, in what context they are done — and again how they are received and built upon, as the means of grace for the life both of the Christian individual and of the Christian community in the world; to speak of the proper upholding of discipline not simply in terms of moral and religious duties and the supervision of them, but also in terms of economic discipline, social discipline, political discipline — and discipline too of the use of time and resources for the church's work in the world. It is helpful to seek to update these Reformed marks of the church; and helpful to keep in touch with them, for they are part of our history; they are sign-posts that tell us where we have been, although it is not so certain that they will continue to be essential as guides to where we are going.

The other set we have to notice, at this point, are the Catholic ones, the ones that in a sense belong to all of us, Roman and Orthodox and Reformed, the ones from the Creed, which declare the church to be marked by its Unity, its Holiness, its Universality and its Apostolicity. Again, we are not short of theologians who seek to update these, and so we are asked to think of the unity of the church more in terms of its mission than of its uniformity; to think of the holiness of the church more in relation to its willingness to follow the self-emptying sacrificial way of Jesus on the Cross, for the sake of the world, than in terms of the more traditional view of holiness, which seems to be to do with 'keeping yourself unspotted from the world'; to think of its universality more in terms of mutual responsibility within the church than in terms of geographical coverage or the application of universal principles; and to think of its apostolicity more in terms of the church's participation in the apostolic (or 'sent out') mission of Christ in and to the world, rather than in a sort of line-management way leading back through the hierarchy to the first apostles.

As with the Reformed marks, so also with the Catholic ones. It is helpful to rethink them from time to time in this way; and on balance they are probably a more important link to retain with what has gone before, if only because they form part of a much larger chain, more battered and bruised and rusted than any other, but still there, holding on. Although I suspect they will always be with us, I do not believe, however, that it will be enough simply to rethink them every now and then; we need to struggle to find new marks in our rapidly changing world, if the church is to remain a living, growing organism, recognisably the Body of Christ in the world.

References
1 Sobrino (1985), p43.
2 Barr (1983).
3 de Santa Ana (1977), p17.

4 de Santa Ana (1977), p21.
5 de Santa Ana (1977), p105.
6 de Santa Ana (1977), p105.
7 United Presbyterian Church (1984).
8 United Presbyterian Church (1984), p12.
9 de Santa Ana (1979), p69.

III

The poor and their story

Who are they?

The subject of this chapter — Who are the Poor, and What is their Story? — must be approached with great caution. Even to put the question at all is to feel oneself terribly exposed, almost, as if one were asking 'Who are the Humans?'; and even to attempt to answer it from outside, as it were, is to lay oneself open to charges of paternalism, partiality and pride — how can I *know* who are the Poor? We must, however, address this question at this point, if we are to get any further along the road of our investigation of the Church and the Poor. For one thing, with the absence of the poor in any recognisable degree from the membership of the church, at least in Scotland and in the Church of Scotland, there is an understandable lack of awareness within the church of their existence and of their story. Individual members and individual ministers will have their own personal experiences, as I have mine, but these do not amount to anything approaching a clearsighted and sympathetic understanding of who the poor are and how they have come to be where they are today. While this is understandable, by no stretch of the imagination can it be excused if we are serious in our proclamation of a Gospel which is good news for the poor. Without wishing to seem irreverent, I sometimes feel that the church's profound ignorance of the life and story of the poor is as incredible as it would have been, for example, if God the Father, seeking to save the human race, had decided to become incarnate — as a dog. Mention of the Incarnation brings me to what would seem to be another extremely important reason for trying, however inadequately, to answer the question — Who are the Poor, and What is their Story? It is all too common, in my experience, for people in church circles to pour scorn on the suggestion that God somehow is specially concerned for the poor. This seems to arise from two sources. On the one hand, church people are inclined to want to broaden, and to spiritualise, the meaning of the word 'poor', until it includes virtually everyone, from the poor — but perhaps quite blissfully happy — village Indian, to the 'poor' — but perhaps quite hellishly miserable — company chairman in London or New York. On the other hand, although closely related to the foregoing, there is a feeling within the church that to suggest God is biased in any way towards any one group or class is somehow not quite playing the game — God is a good chap, and a good chap is surely even-handed and unprejudiced towards everyone?

A place for the poor

Quite simply, the church must be cleansed of these attitudes if it is to make any further progress towards being a place where the poor find a home. As we have already seen the Bible is perfectly clear that the poor have a special place in God's design, that quite clearly the Kingdom of God belongs to them, and not to the rich . . . not because they are poor, but because they live in hope of the coming Kingdom, and do not reckon it is theirs to possess, but rather theirs to receive. The role of the rich is also perfectly clear — they are to hand over the control of their wealth to God, place their hope in Him and in His coming Kingdom, and demonstrate this conversion by placing themselves firmly on the side of the poor. The implications of this clear Biblical teaching are immense and complex, and I do not wish for a moment to suggest that following it out, either for the rich or for the poor, is a simple matter — indeed, as we shall see later, there are very serious doubts as to whether it is even possible to follow it out any more, at least in the West. Let there be no doubt at all as to the commitment of God to the cause of the poor; and let the fundamental Christian doctrine of the Incarnation of God in Christ — born in poverty, thrown into exile when only days old, a man of no worldly wealth and little worldly learning, homeless, misunderstood, rejected, tortured, and killed as a criminal — let belief, therefore, in the Incarnation be the chief foundation on which we take our stand alongside the poor.

It will be a help, at this point, if we can limit the subject. Thus, I am not suggesting that we must reach a final definition of 'the poor' in every age and for all time; such a definition is probably as unattainable, and as undesirable, as the attempt to find the 'ideal' church. Also, for our present purposes, we shall concentrate upon the poor in Scotland, as part of Britain; we shall have occasion to speak also of the poor in the Third World, but only in relation to the poor in this country, which is admittedly grossly unfair to the poor of the Third World, but serves to keep our subject within bounds. Finally, we shall limit discussion in the main to what are known in sociological circles as 'the urban poor' — an ugly phrase, pointing to an ugly perception of a reality which is marked indeed by much ugliness — but by many other characteristics as well.

One criticism often levelled against the Conservative administration in Westminster in recent times is that they have conspicuously failed to demonstrate any feel for what it is like to be poor; one is tempted to suggest, perhaps quite unfairly, that this is because they do not *know* what it feels like in the first place. In a recent compilation by two Scottish Labour MPs on the poor in Scotland, *Scotland: The Real Divide*[1], the first chapter is a well written piece by Scottish novelist William McIlvanney on what it is like to be poor. That chapter, and indeed the whole book are worth reading, for I recognise, especially in McIlvanney's contribution, much that I have observed, and have to a limited extent shared in, over the last twenty years. (Incidentally, so far as I can discover from a careful reading of the whole book, the church is mentioned only once, and then in a critical fashion).

There is not space in this one chapter to give a full description of poverty today. Obviously my own experiences will come through and the reader must make allowances for my prejudiced eye; probably there is no such thing as an unprejudiced eye in this field. Further, one has a certain reluctance to speak too freely of what one has seen and shared — to speak too openly of people with whom one has lived and struggled and celebrated — they are neighbours, friends, colleagues and adversaries and one shrinks from making them, too readily, the objects of a study, however helpful it might appear to be.

Poverty in Scotland

What then, can statistics tell us about poverty today in Scotland? If, to begin with, we take as a top line the level of income which is set by the Government as the cut-off point for eligibility for Supplementary Benefit, and then describe as poor those whose income stands at, or falls below, this level, we may say that the number of the poor in Scotland at the beginning of 1983 amounted to just over one million people — in other words, one in five of the Scottish population. If we add to that figure those who can be described as living on the margins of poverty — the working poor, many pensioners, and others, that figure rises by perhaps a further 650 000; so that we come to a figure for the poor in Scotland amounting to some 1 664 000 or about a third of the population of Scotland. These figures of course fluctuate year by year, but indications are that they are on the increase, rather than the reverse, at the present time. A breakdown of these figures shows, that while the third largest group are single parents, and the second largest are pensioners, by far the largest, in fact nearly half, are people who are unemployed and their dependants[2]. These figures are not perhaps a surprise to you, but they should be a matter of concern for every caring person in the country. It will help to fill them out a little if we note some disturbing trends in Scotland which help to explain how we have reached this parlous condition. It can be shown, for example, that Scotland has moved quite fundamentally in the course of a century from being a nation whose economy was based on manufacturing, to an economy based mainly on service industry. Thus the figures show that in 1851 43 per cent of our workforce was employed in the manufac- turing sector and 16 per cent in the service sector; by 1951 the figures were 25 per cent for manufacturing and 43 per cent for the service sector. Further, in the thirty years between 1951 and 1981, there was a tremendous influx into the Scottish workforce of women, almost all in the service sector, and almost all married women taking part-time jobs; the proportion rising from 30 per cent in 1951 to 43 per cent in 1981[3].

Now let us try to put some flesh and blood on to these disturbing statistics. Professor David Donnison, in his book *The Politics of Poverty*[4] defines poverty as meaning 'a standard of living so low that it excludes people from the community in which they live'. He then goes on, in a very powerful passage, to try to set out what it is like to try to keep your head above water in these conditions:

'To keep out of poverty people must have an income which enables them to participate in the life of the community. They must be able, for example, to keep themselves reasonably fed, and well enough dressed to maintain their self-respect and to attend inter- views for jobs with confidence. Their homes must be reasonably warm; their children should not feel shamed by the quality of their clothing; the family must be able to visit relatives, and give them something on their birthdays and at Christmas time; they must be able to read newspapers, and retain their television sets and their membership of trade unions and churches. They must be able to live in a way which ensures . . . that public officials, doctors, teachers, landlords and others treat them with the courtesy due to every member of the community'.

I am not saying, and I do not think Professor Donnison is saying, that all the million and a half people officially described as living in poverty in Scotland today cannot attain these conditions; everyone is different, even among the poor. Nor is it suggested that the sole reason why so many of them are unable to attain these conditions is because of circumstances totally outwith their control. The poor, like all human beings, can and do make choices — even if they are limited — and sometimes they make the wrong choices. But no-one makes choices in a vacuum. If you are poor, and choose to spend money on a coloured television set rather than on new clothes for the children or a holiday for one week in the year, then it may be because TV helps you, day by day, to escape from the boredom and the frustration of real life, and so helps to keep you sane. If you are poor, and live in a housing scheme on the edge of one of our large cities, and choose to spend money on a tumble-drier when there are those who would say that you should have spent it on decorating your house or tidying up your patch of front garden, then you might want to try to explain to your critics that you cannot hang your clothes in the back green to dry — for there is no back green, and even if there was, you could not be sure that your clothes would still be there when you went out to bring them in. Nothing, it seems, is simple.

But we cannot pass from these statistics, and this experience of poverty in Scotland today, without allowing something of the anger felt by those who observe it, and sometimes who share in it, to come through. I am tempted here to speak of my own experience, especially to speak of my experience as a young, naïve, impressionable divinity student in 1964, finding myself plunged into the dismay and disintegration of life in Gorbals in Glasgow as it finally disappeared, the worst slum in Europe, to re-emerge as the grim, damp, modern redevelopment area of the 1970s. I could tell of the life of the sub-lets, of 60 people crammed into a four-storey tenement building in South Portland Street, with one electric point only on each floor, and one toilet working for the entire building — a building which, incredibly, was down on the list kept by the then Children's Department of the then Corporation of Glasgow, as 'recommended' for temporary accommodation for homeless people. I could tell you of the fight we had to get that building condemned — the fight not just against the Corporation, and the Medical Officer of Health, but also against the respectable Pollokshields lady who turned out to be the owner of the building. Instead, I quote once again the words of David Donnison, formerly Chairman of the Supplementary Benefits Commission for the United Kingdom[6]:

> 'I am moved most fundamentally of all by the plight of poor people. I am disgusted by the depression, deference, fear, jealousy and supercilious comment — all the sick human relationships — which flourish and fester around poverty. When the plight of the poor is contrasted with the wealth and the massive productive capacities which could so readily put things right, I am enraged too. So is everyone who has not lost the capacity for being shocked by injustice. The political reactionaries, the clever professors, the complacent people of middle England who contend, when they argue at all, against the social theories of committed egalitarians are aiming at the wrong target. It is experience, not theory, that moves us. They should instead get out and see the world for themselves'.

I do not seek to lessen in any way the self-authenticating authority of that passage, from a man who should know what he is talking about if anyone does in Britain today, when I say that Isaiah, Amos, and Micah would not have been ashamed to have written these words themselves.

Our task now becomes even more difficult. We have looked briefly at the facts and to some extent the feel of poverty in Scotland today. We have seen that it is a complex matter, that it is a relative matter, but that it is real. What we must now try to do is to discern the story of the poor, for they have a story, and it is vitally important that we try to hear it, at least in outline.

Class division and conflict

The story of the poor in Scotland is the story of the working class, in Scotland and in Britain as a whole. Right away this raises, especially within church circles, the uneasy spectre of class division. I say uneasy because it is my experience, and that of many commentators on the church in modern society, that the concept of class is not one that the church finds easy to handle, let alone to accept as existing at all. Why this is, is not entirely clear. Partly, it may be because church people have been taught to believe that the concept of class division is unacceptable to God and to the Christian faith; that because, as St Paul says, 'there is no difference between Jews and Gentiles, between slaves and free men, between men and women; you are all one in union with Christ Jesus' (Gal.3:28), therefore there ought not to be any talk of class division or any other division when talking about the church in the world.

Leaving aside, for the moment, the blatant fact that, even in spite of Paul's specific words to the contrary, the church has consistently sought to ensure that precisely all these differences continue to exist within the church down through the ages, it is perhaps helpful to note here that, just because the purpose of the church is to demonstrate the dismantling of human barriers, that does not therefore mean that one proceeds by behaving as if the barriers were not there in the first place. On the personal level, there is little point in exhorting a fellow human being (or even yourself, for that matter) to be converted from a life of sin and immorality, if you act on the assumption at the same time that there is in fact no sin, no immorality in your life at all! The other reason — or at least one other reason — why the church is uneasy when it comes to talking about 'class', may be because of its political overtones. To speak of class seems to lead inevitably to speak of class struggle, even of class warfare, and then we are right into areas of life within which the church, especially in this country, feels it must get hopelessly lost — and is therefore extremely cautious about entering.

There is perhaps a certain amount of wisdom in the church's reluctance to enter into the arena of class conflict. As is well known, Marxist theory, and so Marxist practice, works on the assumption that class conflict is an inevitable part of the progress towards the socialist society. We need not here enter into a discussion of the pros and cons of this; suffice it to say that the theory of inevitablity of class conflict is only a theory — and one, moreover, that is challenged very seriously by many commentators.

Though the church is perhaps wise not to align itself with this theory, with all the far-reaching consequences that would flow from it, it is nevertheless necessary to note that, while one can have serious doubts about the inevitability of class conflict and class struggle, one can still recognise the fact that classes do exist, and have always existed, in society — and that classes have their story. This is precisely what we need to do to understand the poor in Scotland today. We need to recognise that they belong to a class; that they have, over the recent century and a half, come to see themselves as part of a class; that they have, over the last 80 years or so, also come to see the point and power of organising themselves as a class to fight for their standard of living, because clearly they were not going to be handed it on a plate; and that, in the course of this whole period, more or less from the beginning of the nineteenth century onwards, they have not in the main seen the church as an ally in their struggle. This is not surprising, for the church has either been an uneasy spectator, seeking often to fudge the issues or to create compromises and reconciliation when neither was appropriate, or else it has been openly on the other side, in spite of a small minority of quite notable exceptions here and there.

Labour and Trade Union Movements

It is difficult — perhaps in fact it is wrong — to try to tell the story of the working class in Scotland, and in Britain as a whole, separately from the birth and growth of the Labour Movement and the Trade Union Movement. As many writers have shown, the growth in the class consciousness of the poor was to a large extent brought about by the efforts of many small groups and individuals to organise and mobilise them for action — for action to improve their own standard of living, and the living standards of their fellows. Tom Johnston, the great Labour Secretary of State for Scotland in the post-war period, wrote a major *History of the Working Classes in Scotland*[7], in which he attempts to trace their story from feudal times right down to the development of the post-war welfare state. It is a moving tale that he tells, especially in the chapter about the church and the working class in the seventeenth and eighteenth centuries, the appalling story of the witch-hunts up and down the land, and in the chapter on the Highland clearances. He clearly sees the working classes of Scotland as having been consistently brutalised and exploited by powerful interest groups, from which neither the feudal barons around Robert the Bruce nor the Reformed Kirk, its Ministers and Kirk Sessions, are excluded nor exonerated.

By the start of the nineteenth century, of course, the industrial revolution was gathering momentum, and as the cities developed, so the poor began, first to trickle, next to flow, and then to flood in through their gates. Society was in no way prepared for what followed; and so, throughout the whole century we see, through the eyes of Dickens and so many other writers, philanthropists, campaigners and even politicians, the frightening and yet at times thrilling struggles for dignity, for better working conditions, and for representation in the growing urban conglomerations of the land. What we do not tend to see so clearly — what, for instance, I was never even invited to look at, at school — is the herculean struggle amongst the poor to pull themselves up by their own bootlaces — an exercise which should not be treated with the contempt it usually attracts.

We cannot here do more than mention some important markers along the way of what could at times be called this *Via Dolorosa* of the poor over the last hundred years. The Chartists of the 1830s and 1840s, had their advanced aims — universal adult male suffrage, vote by ballot, annual Parliaments, abolition of property qualifications for MPs, the payment of MPs, and equal electoral districts — mocked at then, and eventually swamped by forces both internal and external, yet how modest their aims sound today. Chartism rose and fell very fast, but not before it made its mark in Scotland, especially in Paisley where one churchman at least, the Revd Patrick Brewster, Minister of the Second Charge in Paisley Abbey, rose very quickly to leadership of the faction that advocated reform by non-violent means. He was soon swept away, but not before he had stood and defended his advocacy of Chartism before the Presbytery, who suspended him from his duties because of his actions; and his words are perhaps worth noting, if only as a redeeming feature in what is otherwise a sorry tale, as far as the church is concerned. Mr Brewster, Minister, stands before Paisley Presbytery, and speaks to them in this wise[8]:

> 'One Bible, from which was preached the Gospel to the poor, ye
> have shut for a time. One voice, which in humble dependence on
> the Divine Blessing, has been raised for the redress of their many
> grievous wrongs, ye have attempted to silence, but in vain. I
> respectfully tell you, Sir, and this Presbytery, and the Church of
> Scotland, that I shall continue to advocate the rights and the claims
> of the poor, till I see my country emancipated from the iron yoke
> under which it is crushed'.

The 1880s and 1890s throughout Britain saw the real birth of the Socialist and Labour Movements, through the strengthening development of a number of groups and organisations which were eventually to build themselves into the British Labour Party. As you would expect, the formation and development of these groups was in the main the work — often the sacrificial and costly work — of activists, with the broad mass of the people either apathetic or needing to be cajoled and enthused into following. In this connection, some points are perhaps worthy of note in relation to our interest in the gap between the church and the poor. Paul Thompson, in his book *Socialists, Liberal and Labour*[9], published in 1967, claims that secularism was a creed for many of the poor in London, pointing out that in 1885 approximately 30 Secular Societies existed in that city and about 70 in the provinces, although the movement, he notes, seems to have died away by 1897–1900. This point is noted and developed, at the very beginning of the recently published Church of England report on what it calls Urban Priority Areas, *Faith in the City*[10] where one of the reasons given for the alienation of the proletariat from the church in England in the nineteenth centry is that secularists among the proletariat were likely also to be found to be activists in politics and the trade union movement. We shall need to return to this in a moment in order to examine more closely the many other reasons for this alienation of the proletariat from the church at that time, but lest we are tempted to generalise too readily from London out to the whole country, it is perhaps worth quoting the words of an early Labour historian, David Lowe, as they are given in R K Middlemas' book on *The Clydesiders*[11]:

'The Scottish Labour Movement was not founded on materialism ... The instinct for freedom and justice which animated the Covenanters and Chartists also inspired the nineteenth century pioneers. Their heroes were Jesus, Shelley, Mazzini, Whitman, Ruskin, Carlyle, Morris. The economists took second place. The crusade was to dethrone Mammon and to restore Spirit, and to insist that the welfare of the community should take precedence over the enrichment of the handful'.

Certainly, in the last two decades of the nineteenth century, activists were organising the working class in Scotland, and building the momentum for what became virtually a Labour steam-roller amongst the majority of the Scottish population within the first thirty years of the twentieth. We read of crowds of 20 000 at Glasgow Green to demonstrate sympathy with the striking miners in Lanarkshire in 1887, and a smaller crowd of 12 000 in Edinburgh the following week. The Socialist League organiser, J L Mahon, was very busy in the late 1880s, forming local branches all over Scotland, particularly in the East and in the Borders. In 1906 the Glasgow Trades Council were holding classes in industrial legislation and disputes, and directly related political issues, every Wednesday evening, with up to 400 delegates from all the trades and industries of Clydeside attending. In his posthumously published paper, *The Making of a Clydeside Working Class*[12], Calum Campbell follows in fascinating detail the way in which the largely disorganised and highly exploited Lowland, Highland and Irish immigrant labourers of Govan in the last quarter of the nineteenth century, who in the 1870s and 1880s were worse paid, worse housed, and of a shorter life expectancy than virtually every other equivalent group in Scotland, had turned by 1912 into an organised and politically conscious workforce, able to negotiate a better standard of living for itself on every front, and turning in the highest number of labour votes in Glasgow — over 60 per cent.

This rapid and totally inadequate glance at some of the highlights of the story of the working class in Scotland, particularly in the cities, in the latter years of the nineteenth and the early years of the twentieth century, is then the background against which we have to look at the gap between the church and the poor. For some, living through it, it was the creation of a cause. Thus William Morris, the great pioneer socialist, writing on Socialism[13]:

'It is no dream but a cause; men and women have died for it, not in ancient days but in our own time; they lie in prison for it, work in mines, are exiled, ruined for it; believe me, when such things are suffered for dreams, the dreams come true at last.'

Mack, in his study of *The Political Parties in Pollok*[14], gives it as his considered judgement that the best known of the famous Clydesiders, men such as Wheatley, Shinwell, Maxton, Johnston and Buchanan, represented 'a genuinely popular local leadership based largely on manual workers . . . more fully developed in Scotland and the North of England than in the South.'

The Church and the working class
While this cause, this dream or this background was being created — and either participated in or watched, but certainly benefit-

ed from by the poor, the working class — how did the church fare amongst them? I am aware of the many Christian influences that have been clearly seen at work amongst, for instance, some of the early trade unionists and Socialist political leaders, and of the church connections which many of them retained, or even returned to, throughout their struggle; of the genuine concern expressed by many of the clergy, by Church Assemblies, and by many Christian laymen in positions of leadership in politics and in industry and in the realm of social reform; and of the at times heroic involvement by individual church people in the struggle, of which perhaps we may allow Patrick Brewster to be the prototype and standard bearer for the purposes of this rapid sketch of the story. I am also aware of Ted Wickham's damning judgment that the church never lost the working classes, for the church never had them in the first place.

There was, it is true, 100 years ago as there still is today, the opportunity — indeed for many the seeming inevitability — of belonging to a sectarian religious group, especially in the West of Scotland. No matter how you lived or what you did on a Sunday, you were either a Protestant or a Catholic and if you were a Catholic you were much more likely to go to church on Sunday than if you were a Protestant. Sectarian religion of this sort, however, is not the context within which the Gospel of Jesus and His Kingdom for the poor can grow and thrive; and there is evidence, from the 1880s, to show both that employers could abuse sectarianism when it suited them, and also that workers, and not just their leaders, while at times prepared to go along with this abuse if it suited *them*, could also stand out against it in the cause of solidarity and the fight for improved conditions. Thus in 1888 when the largely Catholic dockers of Govan formed the Glasgow Harbour Mineral Workers Union to fight for better conditions, the employers sacked the lot and brought over several hundred labourers from Belfast to replace them, stating in their advertisement that those who applied had to be Protestants. As Calum Campbell notes, this attempt at sectarian bully-boy tactics did not work; in fact, some of the Belfast Protestants refused to blackleg and went home, while others found better paid jobs elsewhere on Clydeside.

Sectarianism is still 'on offer' to the poor, of course. In so far as it appears to package 'religion' in simple, black and white (or rather, orange and green) terms, to infuse it with a sense of group and race solidarity, and to make its practice both undemanding and emotionally satisfying, sectarianism is still 'bought' by many poor families, and even 'sold' to their children. It has, as stated above, little to do with the Kingdom of God as proclaimed by Jesus and the Gospels, and offers no way at all across the gulf between the church and the poor.

The yawning gap

I conclude this chapter with some comments on why the gap between the church and the poor yawned so wide in the late nineteenth century. Professor Smout of St Andrews is the most recent to ask it. He notes, in answer, that 'the working class could no longer see the point of the kind of church they were faced with in the towns and villages of Scotland'; that they found the minister, on the whole, 'hostile or incomprehensible . . . personifying nothing but his obvious middle-class background'; that the old Christian values of 'thrift, restraint and self-improvement' no longer seemed as relevant as before; and that the working class felt increasingly excluded from leadership in the church — even from membership in some cases. He concludes that, with a spirit not so much of open anti-clericalism as of 'canna-be-fashed-ness', a scepticism, a flippancy spreading more widely among the population, the churches increasingly relinquished their wider national and parish vision, and concentrated more and more on their own members — 'so that church membership ultimately became only the hereditary habit that it largely is today'.[15]

In the recent Church of England report already referred to, the reasons for the alienation of the poor from the religious institutions are given, as early as 1851, as being: rented pews, reinforcing social inequalities; deep class divisions in society; a lack of care by the church for the welfare of the poor; a latent anti-clericalism; the sheer grinding fact of poverty (and here we may note one commentator's view that 'the destitute were generally too absorbed in the struggle to remain alive to look for "other-worldly compensations" and if they thought of the Creator at all, they were likely to blame Him for their sufferings'); and lastly the lack of a consistent 'aggressive' mission by the church towards the poor.

Hugh McLeod in his interesting analysis of *Class and Religion in the Late Victorian City*[16], makes two points which, while mainly referring to London, have a wider application: first, that 'to join any sort of church was to mark yourself out as an individualist, someone who, even if liked and respected, was trying to stand out from his neighbours, and might be suspected of looking down on them'; and second, that the more helpless and excluded the poor feel in the world at large, the more they tend to withdraw 'into a more local world, within which their words and actions *were* of some consequence, and questions concerning the general nature of society, let alone the universe, were tended to be dismissed as irrelevant speculations; the arbitrary ruler of the world was not God but Fate'.

For John Kent, writing in the second volume of the WCC's trilogy of the 1970s already noted[17], the crucial issue was that of the redistribution of power. Working class activists saw that this was to be achieved through organisation and struggle, and if necessary through conflict; church leaders saw only the need for schemes of reconciliation which would bind more tightly together the holders and the subjects of social authority. Kent concludes that the various Christian groups (such as the Christian Socialism of F D Maurice, which he sees as having been always 'a middle-class affair, an attitude recommended *to* the working class, but never very popular *in* the working class') concerned about working class life 'were always too sure that they knew what kind of society working class people ought to want; Westcott and his successors were insufficiently interested in what working class people actually *did* want'. He believes that 'these middle-class religious groups had no deep interest in the politics of wages and working conditions which was the normal sphere of trade unionism'. Reconciliation was what the church was after; but it was on the whole an insufficiently costly reconciliation, failing to take with adequate seriousness the whole area of class struggle and class conflict: 'a handful of politically sympathetic middle-class organisations and of locally brilliant parish priests and ministers had no permanent effect on this fundamental distinction between the two worlds, and it is hard to see how it could have done'. Undoubtedly, there were, and there still are, poor people in the churches — but the proportion was, and still is, far fewer than in society as a whole. There were also, and there still are, as we shall go on to see in more detail, attempts to present the Gospel to the poor, to establish a Christian presence amongst the workers; but 'these efforts do not represent a major current in the churches'. Kent's conclusion, confirming that of Wickham and many others, is 'that the underprivileged sections of society have on the whole found no place in the churches and the churches have not seriously tried to welcome them . . . . The ultimate outcome is a vast, solid, structural *separation* between the poor and the churches'.

It is, therefore, in the light of this sort of background, complex and disappointing as it must seem especially from the point of view of the churches, that we must now try to see what has been attempted, in a number of fronts, to bridge the gap between the church and the poor, chiefly since just before the Second World War, in the West and particularly in Scotland — and then to see where we go from here.

References
1 Brown and Cook (1983).
2 Brown and Cook (1983), p28ff.
3 Brown and Cook (1983), p42f.
4 Donnison (1982), p7.
5 Donnison (1982), p8.
6 Donnison (1982), p227f.
7 Johnston (1946).
8 Godfrey and Goldie (1978), p28.
9 Thompson (1967).
10 Church of England (1985).
11 Middlemas (1965), p31.
12 Campbell (1986).
13 Thompson (1977), p306.
14 Middlemas (1965), Introduction.
15 Smout (1986), pp202–208.
16 McLeod (1974), p282.
17 John Kent, 'The Church and the Trade Union Movement in Britain in the 19th Century', in de Santa Ana, (Ed) (1978), pp30–37.

IV

Models for mission

We have been looking so far, briefly and certainly not from every angle, at the gap that exists between the church and the poor, in urban areas of Scotland; and so far the picture has been fairly bleak. My hope in this and succeeding chapters is to examine in some detail attempts that have been made, in the name of the Church and of the Gospel it proclaims as good news to the poor, to bridge that gap. Certainly very important attempts have been made — and it is essential, if we want to learn for the future, that we try at least to assess their successes and failures. Like any other institution, the church climbs forward, if it climbs at all, on the backs of its predecessors; if we are indeed to climb, and not just remain stranded on a platform that we should have left years ago, or worse still slide backwards, then we must learn from the past.

The Church with the poor
In these next two chapters, then, let us try to see what I shall call 'the church *with* the poor', and let us look at Parish Mission, both in practice and in theory, as it has been attempted and reflected upon, both in Scotland and in the World Church. Before we start, let me make a necessary limitation to this survey.

There have been, and still are, many attempts to be the church with, or alongside, the poor, which have been and are being made by Christian groups and communities who stand outwith what we know as the 'mainline' churches. I am thinking, of course, of the many Missions, Free Churches, and loosely organised groupings which have always existed, and which it seems have increased both in numbers, and in many cases in effectiveness, in recent years. It would indeed be unjust were it to be thought that I regard them as irrelevant, because I do not deal with them in these chapters. I think there are important things to learn from them, although it is clearly not to be assumed that they were, in the main, more successful than the mainline churches in bridging the gap. Sometimes they were, sometimes they were not — and this is still the case. Hugh McLeod, in his study of *Class and Religion in the Late Victorian City*[1], referring to London, raises the interesting question why it was that 'working men did not respond to exclusion from the major denominations by forming their own sects, and why such bodies as the Primitive Methodists and the Salvation Army were even weaker in London than the Anglicans and the Wesleyans', and it will be the interesting subject of some other study to compare and contrast the Missions and groups in Scotland with the mainline churches, both in their success in bridging the gap and in the nature of the Gospel they took with them and planted amongst the poor of the country.

Parish missions and Thomas Chalmers

I shall focus here upon the mainline churches, and specifically on the Church of Scotland and to a lesser extent on the Church of England, for two reasons. The first, clearly, is because I speak from within one such mainline church and therefore I must play to my strength, as it were, and not to my many weaknesses. My second reason is this: the mainline churches, for all their faults and failings, seek nevertheless to hold to the whole Gospel, for the whole people, in the whole world. That this is an endeavour fraught with immense difficulties, profound tensions, and may even be a task impossible of fulfilment, does not detract, in my view, from the fundamental rightness of its approach. The history of the Christian church is littered with divisions, most of which have resulted from a combination of historical and personal differences, and from the conviction that the mission of the church at any particular time can best be served by a parting of the ways. With hindsight, it may be possible to say whether this was, or was not, the case; and I do not hold to the view that unity, sometimes thinly disguised as uniformity, must be preserved at all costs. However, the direction of the Gospel is towards wholeness and not towards divergence and differentiation; the temptation to split off and 'do your own thing', however strong at times it may be, and however convinced one may be of the impossibility of sticking with the main body of the church, is to be struggled against very strongly on every occasion. In the most important divisions within the church, let it be said, this has normally been the case; reforming, or renewing, or even frankly alternative groups have not so much left as been kicked out, struggling and protesting, from the body of the main. This in truth is how it should be, and until that happens, if happen it must, our duty is to hold to the main, and hold fast with everything we have got.

The story of Parish Mission in Scotland might begin, at least in modern times, with Thomas Chalmers. Chalmers came to the Tron Church in Glasgow in July 1815, fresh from a happy and reasonably effective ministry in the rural parish of Kilmany. Within a few months, he had sized up the situation in his new parish with remarkable accuracy and in great detail. Glasgow, at that time, was in the grip of a serious economic depression following the ending of the long period of war against the Continental powers, and was also suffering from a huge influx of poor people from Ireland and the surrounding countryside, as the industrial revolution gathered steam. The Church of Scotland, however, remained strangely silent on the frightening social issues that were rapidly being thrown up in the city; there were nowhere nearly enough churches for the rapidly growing population; the policy of high seat rents in such churches as did exist meant, inevitably, that the seats were filled mainly with those who could afford to pay; there was no system of church schools; and poor relief was mainly in the hands either of the Town Hospital, accountable to the Town Council, or of voluntary charitable societies, who in 1815 contributed £20 000 to the cause, compared to a paltry £2000 from the Church. Furthermore, the Church of Scotland distributed such poor relief of its own as was available, not through individual Kirk Sessions, but through a General Session of the Church, which was by no stretch of the imagination a sufficiently flexible system to meet the growing and crying needs of the poor.

Chalmers surveyed this scene; he looked at his own parish, noting that there were some 10 000 souls within its bounds, of whom about one in a hundred came to church; he compared, naturally, the strong sense of parish community he had left behind in Kilmany with the almost complete absence of communal spirit which he found in Glasgow; and he concluded that the parish system, in the city, had, in his own words, 'broken up'.

His response was energetic, strategic, and immediately effective. First, he conducted a personal visitation of his parish, street by street, home by home. The immensity of this very task alone is impressive and although he soon felt quite overwhelmed by the sheer size of the job that confronted him, he learned from it some vital lessons. He learned, for a start, that he was looked upon mainly as an agent of the various charitable organisations and welcomed primarily as someone who might be able to produce cash on the nail. This led him very rapidly to dissociate himself from these organisations for he was determined that his parishioners should see him only as their parish minister, with no economic strings attached. The warm welcome he nevertheless received in so many homes, where a representative of the Kirk had perhaps never been seen before, taught him, as he put it, 'the greatest respect for the people' — and a love for them which he never lost. By far the most important lesson he learned, however, was that he could do little on his own.

So he turned to his congregation in the Tron. He turned, specifically, to the Kirk Session. Ordaining twenty new, young, middle-class elders, he trained them to see themselves as primarily agents of the church within the parish and set them to house-to-house visitation, urging upon them the necessity of using their own financial means, if necessary, to alleviate the poverty they found there. Not content with that, he then proceeded to institute a parish educational programme, creating the Tron Parish Sabbath School Society, and insisting, in order to prevent it from being swamped by children only from the congregational families, that they should keep their classes small, and enrol only parish children.

These activities, as might be expected, met with some opposition from sections within his own congregation, particularly those who saw their minister as called to fulfil the role primarily of chaplain to the congregation. However, Chalmers stuck to his guns; not only in his activities within the parish, but also in his preaching within the congregation, he laid out before them his concept of the 'godly commonwealth', and the duty, as he saw it, of the church to seek to strive to 'transform society into a godly commonwealth of Christian communities'. He also, again to his credit, saw and preached against the anti-Roman Catholicism of many Protestants, believing this to be both irrational and unfair; although it has to be said that his missionary endeavours amongst the poor of Glasgow, while offering help to all irrespective of their denomination, were not organised, nor could they in all fairness have been expected to be, on an inter-denominational basis.

Firmly committed to a view of society which was essentially rural in background, and to a view of the church which was primarily benevolently paternal in action, Chalmers strove to develop a system of church life and action in early nineteenth century Glasgow which would work through small, tight-knit Christian communities, under the supervision of parish church and parish school, discovering for themselves a revitalised Christianity, industry, and benevolence. He continued this approach when he went to St John's in the early 1820s, reviving the office of deacon in order to supervise poor relief in each of the twenty-five elders' districts in the new parish. Suspicious of, and hostile to, the new state system of dealing with poor relief, which he saw as setting up the conditions for conflict between rich and poor, and leading the poor to seek help, not from the church, but from the state, he struggled to hold on to the old, rural, communal-based system of care for the poor through the church alone. In St John's, he succeeded in his aim, but the means by which he attained it raised serious questions. They were highly paternalistic — and failed to take into account both the human failings of his own deacons and his own poor, and to reckon with the immense social forces which were even then gathering momentum within the working class. His helpers were all outsiders, who never had any intention of even trying to become members of the local parish community; the poor never apparently even imagined they were being invited to become members of a new sort of Christian commonwealth — and continued quite happily to accept the hand-outs when they could.

Stewart J Brown, to whose study of Chalmers I am much indebted, makes this judgment[2]:

'His godly commonwealth ideal offered a communal alternative to the social anxieties and suffering of early industrialisation — a turning backward to an idealised past, when, he assured the nation, the social orders had lived in communal harmony, and sacrificed together for common ideals represented by a national Covenant with God'.

He was an individualist with a strong sense of the importance of community — but of the rural sort — who believed in the centrality of the reformation of the individual character, through preaching, through parish visitation, through benevolent paternalism, and through parish schools.

Looking back at Chalmers in amongst the poor, across the space of one and half centuries, it is astonishing how much one recognises, and how much has not changed: the breakdown of the parish system within the city; the view of the church and its full-time officials as primarily channels of charity within a one-way system of hand-outs; the energetic and imaginative approach of the 'new young minister', especially in his use of the Kirk Session and of new elders to work within the parish; the work with the children; and even the tension that his parish-orientated ministry created amongst his congregation, especially with those who saw him as their chaplain first and foremost. Any minister today who has experience of going to work in an inner-city parish and congregation will have not the slightest difficulty in recognising all of this, and will want, as I do, to see in Thomas Chalmers a brother and a fellow-fighter on the way, and to salute him for his courage and his imagination and his style.

We could salute him too for his vision, but the fact remains that it never got beyond a vision — the vision of the church as the caring community, in which the poor found a true home, and all barriers were broken down between man and God and between man and man. Chalmers has been accused of many things: of benevolent paternalism; of social engineering; of adherence to a totally inadequate theory of population control; and of attempting to build a national campaign for social reform based on one limited local experiment which had been produced by doubtful means, and had achieved questionable results. To all of these accusations, the verdict has been one of guilty; but we must say more. For instance, we must ask how far was it even likely that his vision could have been achieved, when the social world of the parish church had already become the religious equivalent of the social world of the well-to-do, of the growing merchant class of nineteenth century Glasgow and their circle? How likely was it to have been achieved, when the poor were seen, by Chalmers as much as by his congregation, as the objects of both their charity and of the Gospel — the consumers, if you like, of the goods, both spiritual and material, of which he wanted the church to be the sole producer and distributor in the world? How likely was it to have been achieved, in the face of the forces which were already at work in the world of nineteenth century Glasgow — forces which were already laying the foundations for the deep divisions within society which were to become one of the main features of social and political, and religious, life right down to the present day?

A fraternal, admiring and humble salute, then, to Thomas

Chalmers — with the prayer too that he will forgive us if our judgment, from the great distance and with the benefits of hindsight, seems unduly harsh. To his perfectly understandable, if hypothetical, question — 'Well, show me what *you* have done?' — we do not, perhaps, have too ready, or nearly as impressive, goods to display.

We now turn to another part of Glasgow and to another century — in fact, to Govan in the 1930s — to find a situation, a minister and an analysis which at first sight differs very little from what we have just described. In his booklet, with the unwieldy title *Are Not the Churchless Million Partly the Church's Fault?*[3] George Macleod, Minister of Govan Old Parish Church from 1930 to 1938, describes a situation which Thomas Chalmers would have recognised all too well. Just to give the headings of the sections of his first chapter is enough to set the scene: The advantages of the parish system; What is the parish system?; The parish system breaks down; The spiritual results of the break-down; the churchless millions; it is all there, even in outline form. In 1932, speaking at a Church of Scotland Forward Movement Congress in Glasgow[4], Macleod put the problem in typically dramatic form:

'The Church is failing hopelessly to affect or to appeal to the people in their thousands around the doors, and I say it in full responsibility that at the present moment in this city, not because we want it, but because we cannot help it, the churches we are closing down are the churches in the poorest areas, because they are not paying. There is a dying to be done by every single one of us, a dying to the idea that the minister's sole job is to go round the people who are of the redemption already, a recovery of the view that the congregation and its minister are in the centre of their parish as leaven for the lump'.

Surveying his new parish in 1930, as Chalmers surveyed his in 1815, Macleod found, and concluded from his findings, much the same as Chalmers. He found a parish of 650 contiguous Protestant households, of which only 175 had some definite church connection, and further, that only ten of these households were connected with Govan Old Parish Church, the remaining 165 being connected with no fewer than 23 churches scattered throughout the city. He concluded that 'the Church is ... cut off from one of the primary conditions of its health, which is that it should always be looking outward if it is to retain inward poise . . . and seeks in vain for an area which it can proceed to leaven'. He concludes, further, that 'there is an element of Confucianism that has strangely gotten hold of many Presbyterians — a resolve to worship at irregular intervals at the tomb of their ancestors — they would rather miss four communions than "lift their lines" from the place where their fathers never dreamt of missing one!' What the church should therefore be concerned with, he wrote, is 'the outward organisation of the Church, in default of whose better ordering none of these differing emphases' — the style of worship, social concern, or a return to a purer preaching of the Word — 'are likely permanently to hold the masses whom we have lost. We are concerned, that is, with the system of the propagation of the Gospel, within a closely compacted nation, the large majority of whose citizens claim nominal allegiance to her national church'.[5]

Missionary outreach and George Macleod

With the energy and organisational ability which has been, and remarkably still is, some 50 years later, one of the hallmarks of this remarkable man, Macleod set about doing something about the situation he had so clearly perceived. His aim was straightforward. The parish church, with all its resources and above all with its clear Gospel faith in the 'good news' for the whole person in the whole world, must now mobilise itself in order to 'bring back' the thousands around its doors who had lapsed from the faith, and who were, he firmly believed, just waiting to be asked back in. The 'leaven' was to get out there in amongst the 'lump', and do its work. The result was the famous Mission of Friendship of 1933-34, which was to prove a model for Parish Mission in Scotland, not just for his time, but in many respects right down to the present day. Throughout the winter of 1933, and on into the spring of 1934, he set about a Mission to the congregation, some 50 per cent of whom lived outside the parish area, culminating in a Witness of Loyalty and special Dedication Services at Easter 1934 — the aim being to strengthen the faith and the sense of mission within the congregation as a prelude to going out into the parish. Immediately this first phase of his Two-Year Plan was ended, the second phase swung into operation — preparation for a Mission — or Message — of Friendship to the whole parish, with visitors going round every door two or three times, two by two, during the summer and early autumn, and culminating in what can only be described as a 'blockbuster' of a week of Missionary Outreach from 21 to 28 October 1934. Anyone who lived through that week — and there are still those who speak of it today — could not have failed to be affected, some more powerfully than they can say, even yet. Draughtsmen from the shipyards prepared and drew posters which created and heightened the sense of expectancy already raised by the visitations. In the church, a chain of prayer continued daily from ten in the morning until eight at night. In the church vestibule, hundreds of booklets and leaflets on every aspect of church life were sold every day. Each afternoon, several streets were visited and short meetings held — in the pouring rain! Never one to miss a chance for the visual and the symbolic in the presentation of the faith, Macleod stormed round the parish carrying a Celtic bell, a pastoral staff, an open Bible and a banner specially prepared for the event. At five each afternoon thousands of children came to the church and the Pearce Institute straight from school to attend special children's events — not to play games, but 'to hear the salient facts of our redemption preached'. Then at 7.00 *pm* teams took their stand at three open-air stances in the parish, for street-preaching without questions, streaming thereafter into the church behind the robed boys' choir, to hear the Missioner, the Revd Robin Scott, preach the Gospel and call them to conversion and to prayer. Nor was the day finished even yet, for the crowds — and crowds there really were — divided then by sexes, the women to hear a returned woman missionary from China, the men to take part in 'Question Time', where everything from the Social Gospel and the Peace Witness of the church to the significance of the Book of Daniel and the salary of the Archbishop of Canterbury were subjected to loud and rigorous questioning until 10.30 *pm*. On the final evening, again in the pouring rain, they made a final round of the whole parish, stopping at well-defined points, singing as they went, speaking of the Gospel to all and sundry, both Catholic and Protestant, appealing to all 'good Christians to bestir themselves and return to their own church allegiance and there learn the Message of Friendship to all mankind'.

The immediate results cannot fail to impress. Over 200 children joined the Sunday School; over 100 came forward with old church lines; 220 people joined a New Communicants' class, of whom only 20 fell away; over 80 came forward for adult baptism. All this, as he says, 'in response to the Church of Scotland in the process of what should clearly be its normal activity'. Macleod was not afraid to recognise the limitations, however, of this achievement; even two years after the event he writes:

'As a church we were not as a whole ready for this response, and the process of consolidation continues and is by no means complete. As a staff . . . we were too faithless of the measure of the co-operation [of their fellow-workers in the congregation], and thereby condemned ourselves to patchy following-up, for which we alone were gravely to blame'.

His conclusion stated with all the supreme confidence which was, and still is, his hallmark, his great strength and, dare one say it, possibly also his Achilles' heel, was this:

'Our primary conviction was proved to the very hilt. The Churchless Million is largely the blame of the Church herself, and, until we set our house in order, we dare not blame one single soul. If only she would lift up her eyes and look into the fields, she would find them still ripe unto harvest. If the Church cares even now to take her serious part, the answer of Scotland for Christ is as certain as the dawn'.[6]

The reader will readily appreciate the sense of disloyalty I feel when I now go on to question his methods and his confidently proclaimed conclusions, not just for Govan, but for the whole of Scotland. I am one of his sucessors as minister of Govan Old; I have been a member for over twenty years of the Community he founded; and personally I owe more to George Macleod, in almost every way that matters to a man, than I owe to any other single living soul. However, some questions must be asked; indeed, I take some courage from the conviction I have that he too would want to ask them.

I believe, to begin with, that when he looked out at Govan he saw to a certain extent what he wanted to see. Certainly he saw the unemployed and the destitute and the despairing in their thousands; not only saw them, but loved them, spoke to them, argued with them, and served them, and there are scores if not hundreds in Govan and indeed throughout the world today who bear witness, as I know from personal and often very moving experience, to the good work Macleod and his team did amongst the poor of the Depression days, not only during these two years of the Mission of Friendship, but throughout the whole eight years of his ministry there. I do not in any way wish to detract from the immense effect of this work, nor to suggest that all the things he set going — the workshops for the unemployed, the development of the gardens, the rebuilding of Fingalton Mill out in the country as a place for recreation away from the city slums, the raising of a political and social consciousness within many in the church — that all this did not contribute to the 'preaching of the Gospel' in a most real and lasting way. Nevertheless, it must be said that he left the structure still unchanged, and left unchallenged the view, held by Chalmers in 1815, and still held firmly by many, perhaps by most in the Church of Scotland today, that the structure is all right if only it can be made to work, and that the people outside are simply waiting to be asked 'back in'. He did not, it seems, find it possible to conduct his Mission on an inter-denominational basis — even though he was soon to become a leading exponent of ecumenical co-operation at all levels, as his famous pamphlet of the 1950s, *Bombs and Bishops*[7] so clearly showed.

What I am saying is that this will not do. It did not do then, and I suspect he glimpsed as much, even in the midst of the excitement and the power of the Mission of Friendship. It is fairly easy, from this distance, to see how he failed really to seek to understand what made some of the people of Govan — the Churchless Million, or part of it — really tick; how he too readily assumed that they were all waiting, sheep without a shepherd, to be drawn back into the fold. It is easy too now to ask sharp questions about the fact that, at the end of the tremendous effort over two years, fewer than 300 people actually moved 'back', or even in some cases 'forward' into traditional church membership; and to recognise even in his own assessment of the Mission a sense that he was going to have great difficulty in holding them within the structures of the congregation as it was still constituted in Govan Old. Is it too unkind a judgment to say that, in the Mission of Friendship of 1933–34, what Macleod was doing was the old thing supremely well — and that what was really needed was some new thing, of which he perhaps had already glimpsed a partial vision, however inadequately, and however tentatively, himself? In November 1935, only a year after the Mission was ended, there appeared a paper, written for private circulation by Macleod, which sets out in some detail his proposals for the founding of the Iona Community, in which he seems to recognise that more was needed than doing the old thing well. In this paper, for which I am indebted to my late father-in-law, the Very Revd Hugh O

C

Douglas, who served with Macleod as one of his Assistants in Govan in the 1930s, Macleod spells out his conviction that what the church needs to rediscover above all in the modern world is 'community' — the sense of brotherhood, of life together, a bridging of the gap between the church and the unemployed, not through Missions of Friendship, however well organised, but through experiment in living together, and in working together, so that, in his own words, 'each would learn from the other of a church that was setting its sails to a new pattern — albeit to catch the same breezes that first brought Iona's Message to the Mainland'. This, as I say, he was spelling out in 1935, and in such advanced and detailed form that it is hard to believe it had not been forming in his mind over the past couple of years at least — in other words, while the Mission of Friendship was going on. It was to be another three years before the vision began to take shape, with his founding of the˘Iona Community and the commencement of the rebuilding of Iona Abbey in 1938; and even then, and in fact even yet, I do not think we can say that the vision has been fully seen or fully grasped by the Community, never mind by the church at large. However, it points in a direction — in the direction of community, not imposed from above, but growing up from below, community forming in dialectical tension between the church, the world, and the Gospel — and it is in this direction, I believe, that the church and the world must go, if the gap is to be bridged at all.

Anticipating the Mission of Friendship
Before we leave Macleod and Govan in the thirties it is interesting to note a precursor of his Mission of Friendship, to which he was directly indebted, and to hear a judgment on it from one who was involved. In the years directly before the outbreak of the First World War, 1912-13, in the Parish of Portsea in Plymouth, almost the exact prototype of Macleod's Mission of Friendship twenty years later was carried out, with almost exactly the same results. There was the Two-Year Plan; the Mission to the Congregation; the visitation of the homes; the Ten Days Mission of Friendship, with many of the same activities that Macleod carried out in Govan — the chain of prayer, the open-air services with the robed choirs, the processions round the streets, the packed meetings, the children's services, and the closing services in the church. Indeed, it seems that the Portsea mission differed from the Govan Mission

in virtually only one respect; the weather was fine throughout! The Vicar of Portsea, under whose energetic direction the Mission was conceived and conducted, was the Revd Cyril Garbett, better known for his later role as Archbishop of York in the Church of England. Writing many years later, in his 1952 book *In an Age of Revolution*[8], Garbett has this to say about the mission in Portsea:

'In the interval between the wars there were many local evange-listic efforts; it was, however, becoming plain that the old-fashi-oned ten-day parochial mission was no longer the converting agency it had been in the past; it taught and strengthened the faithful, but it won few who were not already Christians. When Vicar of Portsea I had a mission for the parish . . . . Large numbers of resolution cards were signed, and many who had lapsed from the Church returned, but the number of those who had been altogether outside the Church and who were converted by the mission was extremely small. This has been the general experience in the years between the wars'.

Nowadays, what we are hearing more and more — and the words are true, and worthy of our serious attention — is that the church must not think of Mission as a one-off thing, but rather as the whole purpose of its being in the world. Mission must be continuous; in the words of a Church of Scotland pamphlet[9], introducing the Programme for Action of the Church in the 1980s, one of the basic needs of the church today is stated as missionary congregations who look beyond their family circles and their buildings, who go out into the community around in friendship, service and witness, and share in the world-wide mission of the church. I am concerned — and I believe the church in general should be concerned — that even now, even with our seemingly deepened understanding of the continuous nature of mission, even in the face of the experience of the intensive and powerful activities of men like Chalmers and Macleod, we are still thinking that we can bridge the gap by somehow strengthening the old structures which have served well in the past and can surely serve well for all time to come. The witness of men like Garbett and Macleod, however tentative, however compromised, cannot surely be avoided; this will not do.

Is this all that can be tried? Indeed not; and in the next chapter we shall look at further examples of attempts to bridge the gap between church and poor, in the House Church movement, in the mobilisation of the whole congregation for mission (in particular in Tom Allan's famous North Kelvinside experiment in Glasgow in the 1940s), and in the thinking of the wider church in Scotland, in England and in the World Council of Churches.

References
1 McLeod (1974), p282.
2 Brown (1982), p371f.
3 Macleod (1936).
4 From a Press report of the Church of Scotland Forward Movement Congress in Glasgow in 1932.
5 Macleod (1936), p12ff.
6 Macleod (1936), p24.
7 Macleod (1957).
8 Garbett (1952).
9 Church of Scotland (1980).

V

A missionary church

An official evangelist

In this chapter we shall examine some more attempts at relating the church to the poor, both in practice and in theory, this time coming more up to date, nearer our own time. Mention has already been made of Tom Allan's book *The Face of My Parish*[1], published in 1954, which described and reflected upon the Parish Mission which he carried out in his North Kelvinside parish in Glasgow in the years immediately following the end of the Second World War. He came to his parish, a mainly working class area of some 10 000 souls, in 1946, and like Chalmers and Macleod before him very quickly realised that a huge gap existed between the people in his congregation and the people of his parish. Doing his analysis, he reckoned that, of the 10 000, perhaps only 100 of his members lived within the area. Reflecting with concern on this situation, he found his preliminary conclusions confirmed by Cyril Garbett in his book, already referred to,[2] 'Religion is now the concern of a small section of the people; its claim for the whole of life is no longer made with any confidence, and only very rarely treated as serious'.

Allan's response was to call in the Revd D P Thomson, a well known evangelist who, since the war, had become the official Evangelist of the Home Board (now Department of Ministry and Mission) of the Church of Scotland. Thomson and Allan organised a Mission in the parish starting with a visitation of the whole area by a team formed from people from outwith the congregation. Following this up, they then led a campaign from within the membership of the congregation; 50 visitors, going out every evening for a fortnight, after a meal and a communion service together, to do door-to-door visitation, with the aim of offering friendship to all, conducting a census of church involvement, distributing literature, inviting people to come to church and 'witnessing to Christ'.

The results were impressive, and far-reaching. Immediately, over 100 people joined his congregation, of whom 50 came in for the first time; the Sunday School doubled its numbers, and every congregational organisation showed an increase. Furthermore, many members of the congregation were enabled, often after initial reluctance, to see their role as members of a missionary church in a quite new light. Allan says[3]: 'I began to see the meaning of the missionary church, and realised for the first time the compelling power of the redeemed community'. However, by far the most important result of the whole experience was that it led Allan to reflect honestly and imaginatively on the major difficulty that the very success of the Mission brought into sharp relief: the problem of the assimilation of the incoming members into the existing congregational pattern of the church.

Joining the church

Mention has already been made of this problem in an earlier chapter. In Allan's words[4], 'it is the easiest thing in the world to get people to "join" the church; it is supremely difficult to know what to do with them once they are in; and it is virtually impossible to keep the majority of them within the conventional framework of the church's life'. We must remember that this was taking place in the years immediately post-war; that there was a real sense of a 'new beginning' in the country; that servicemen and women were settling back into civilian life; and that the church was still there, and, in North Kelvinside, making a consistent and lively attempt to welcome people back in. Nevertheless, Allan found himself, at the end of his Mission, ministering to two virtually separate congregations — those who had always been there, and those who had 'come in' — and the gap between them was quite large. What was he to do? He examined in some detail one possible answer, formed in France from the experience of the Worker-Priest movement and the 'Mission de Paris', both of which were, by 1954, when the book was written, in the process of dissolution by the Roman Catholic Hierarchy; he rejected, however, what he found there — in Godin's words[5] 'the founding of small Christian communities living in the milieu and radiating Christianity from their very midst' — and we shall have to look in more detail at why he rejected this approach later on. His own answer, based on his firm conviction that the congregation, for all its faults and failings, still had to be the main channel of mission within the parish, was to seek to develop new patterns of life within the congregation, beginning with the small nucleus of members who had been fired up and bound tightly together by the experience of the Mission that he and Thomson had conducted. His experience had also confirmed his belief that the only way to prepare a church for mission was by actually doing mission — that it was quite wrong to think first that the congregation had to be cleansed and strengthened before setting about reclaiming the lapsed and challenging the careless.

Convinced of the importance of the place of the lay person in the missionary outreach of the church, he set about building up the personal and corporate life of his small nucleus, what he calls 'the church within the church'. He started with weekly meetings, open to all, with an average attendance of 50, doing Bible Study, discussing common concerns, and sharing in worship, with frequent Communion. These large meetings soon split down into smaller 'cells' meeting in houses, and coming together frequently; in fact, House-Churches in all but name. At the time of the writing of the book, these groups were still in existence, and still seemed to Allan to be the best way of opening both the congregation and the parish to the empowering action of the Holy Spirit — both for themselves as individuals, and for the building up of the whole Body of Christ in the parish.

He did not remain unaware, however, of the difficulties that their very existence posed for the church as a whole. He saw, with commendable honesty, that they could become divisive, exclusive, even Pharasaical, the focus for cranks, and introverted; and asked the fundamental question — to which unfortunately it seems he offered no answer — as to how far such groups are practicable or even legitimate within the framework of the conventional pattern of the church's life, as it presently existed. Despite these very serious problems, Allan remained convinced that this was the way forward; that even although it meant tension, conflict and misunderstanding, 'the gulf between the parish and the church is being bridged', and 'it reminds us that the way of Christian discipleship is still the way of a Cross'.[6]

As will be discussed later, Allan's experience was to be formative on a much wider front in Scotland, and not just among the poor, as he applied it, with great effect, within the Tell Scotland Movement. In his conviction of the importance of the total missionary task of the local congregation; in his view that it is in the doing of mission that progress alone can be made; in his recognition of the importance of community, of personal evangelical commitment, and of small Christian cells within the congregation and parish, based primarily on the lay person; and last, but by no means least, in his recognition of the tensions and difficulties that this approach raised; in all this, the whole church is much in his debt. The fundamental problems, however, still remain. The huge gap, both cultural and personal as well as in terms of acceptance of the Faith, still yawns between the church and the world; the structural fundamentalism of the church, as we have already seen, remains firmly impervious to change, even when such change is worked at with the enthusiasm and inspiration of a D P Thomson and a Tom Allan; all the problems of alienation, recognised by Allan and Michonneau, and later by Sissons and so many others, were not overcome. Influenced as he was so deeply by Michonneau's book *Revolution in a City Parish*, Allan must have agreed with his French colleague that the thousands of souls outwith the church in his parish were '"Christifiable" but not yet "Ecclesiasticable"'[7]; the key word in that admittedly rather clumsy but nevertheless revealing phrase is the word 'yet', for it reveals what is the fundamental weakness of both Allan's and Michonneau's approach. They remained convinced that these souls would eventually come into the church, would, one day, come in as a result of the faithful and corporate activity of the renewed Christian congregation. Quoting the French lay theologian Jacques Ellul, Allan obviously approves of his belief that the renewed Christian congregation, undertaking a 'search for a new "style of life"' for itself, will 'engage in a work which aims at rebuilding parish life, at discovering Christian community, so that people may learn afresh what the fruit of the Spirit is'.[8]

Attractive and impressive as this approach still sounds — and indeed as it is still practised and commended by the Church of Scotland to this very day — one has to ask the question — is the existing ecclesiastical set-up, however renewed and enthused, the best place to begin? Undoubtedly it seems the logical place to begin; after all, as Allan and Michonneau both insist, it is *there*. However, in the very manner, style and internal context of its being there, it seems to keep on erecting, or confirming, more barriers than it can break down; and if we keep on, indeed if we pursue with zeal and enthusiasm, the path of renewal and reformation of the existing set-up, are we not in danger of hindering the very Spirit whom we seek to follow, who may in fact already be 'out there' in a quite different way, 'finding new ways to touch the hearts of all'? We tread here on very thin ice indeed; we cannot just go back and start again; and even to try to follow the Spirit out of the present ecclesiastical structures is to lay ourselves open, as we shall see very shortly, to almost as many dangers as seeking to remain within them and trying to reform and renew them, hopefully and in obedience to the same Spirit. Nevertheless if, as Tom Allan says — and who can deny it? — 'the way of Christian discipleship is still the way of a Cross', then we cannot at least avoid asking the question — is there not a 'dying to be done' to the view that the old ways can be made to work if they are renewed, and to the approach to a bridging of the gap which *starts* from within the church, rather than from out there in the world?

House-Church movement

To these uncomfortable and confusing questions, we shall have to return. For the moment with all too much haste, we must move on to look at another attempt to bridge the gap — this time, the House-Church movement. The Revd Ernest Southcott, who was Vicar of the Anglican Parish of Halton in Leeds at much about the same time as Tom Allan was Minister in North Kelvinside in Glasgow, came to many of the same conclusions as Allan as far as the bridging of the gap was concerned, and he went further than Allan mainly in the greater detail and width of his development of the 'Christian Cell' within the congregation as the crossing point between the church and the world — the House-Church. 'When the congregation meets by dozens in dispersion in five or ten houses of regular worshippers', he writes in his book *The Parish Comes Alive*, published in 1956[9], 'to study the Bible, to pray together, to discuss together and to be concerned about their neighbourhood, the church becomes the church in a way it can never do at the parish Church'. Like Allan, Southcott is convinced of the importance of the parish system and the congregation within it as the focus of mission; like Allan, he is certain that what the church, at congregational level, needs to recover is a sense of community; and also like Allan, he is sure that they will not do this unless, at the same time, they actually *do* mission. The formation of his house-churches, meeting either in the homes of members of the congregation — what he calls the intensive house-church — or in the homes of people who are not regular worshippers — the extensive house-church — makes for compulsive reading; and many church denominations and groups followed his lead, and still do today, to such an extent that there now even exists in England, and to a much smaller extent in Scotland, a type of church structure based on house-churches which is virtually an alternative to the mainline churches. It is, however, mainly middle-class in composition, and as such reflecting little more than a different way of reaching out to, and nurturing in life and faith, the group with whom the churches have always been most successful; it offers little by way of helping us to bridge the gap which still exists between the church and the poor. It is still based on the conviction that, as Southcott puts it,[10] 'the church is called to *bring to the world* the fullness, the wholeness of Christ,' to offer to the world 'a quality of life . . . which the world cannot find elsewhere'. John Robinson, writing in the magazine *Theology* in August, 1950, and quoted by Southcott in his book, makes what perhaps might be described as the highest claims for the House-Church movement, when he says that 'the house-church represents, so to speak, the tap-roots of the vine, the Church underground, that of the life of the tree most closely in contact with the clinging soil of every day existence: it is the tree as it is embedded in the deepest crevices and seams of the secular world'. Nourished and fed by what flows through the house-church, Robinson then sees, with splendid and yet highly revealing imagery, 'the parish church . . . throwing out its leaves and fruit in the great dioceses and provinces which cover the earth, and rearing its head in the heavenly places as the "general assembly and church of the first-born"'.[11]

The problem which the House-Church movement of Southcott leaves unanswered — and, unlike Allan, largely unrecognised — is that it is based on the assumption that what has to be done is to go out and find a new way of bringing people into the existing structures of the church. Neither Allan or Southcott, of course, is suggesting that the existing structures are perfect; both are excited by the way in which their experiments in outreach are actually changing the attitudes of their own existing members to what being a Christian, and being a member of a Christian community, means in the world of today. Both of them, Allan perhaps less than Southcott, fail to come to close quarters with what seem to me to be the two fundamental problems inherent in their approach; which are, first of all, that if the church is failing to bridge the gap, then it is always seen as the church's fault, and the church must be renewed but not necessarily radically altered; and, second, that the people 'out there' are, not to put too fine a point on it, just waiting for the church to find the right approach in order to be able to 'come in'. They are not alone in holding these views, but both the facts of history and the facts of faith raise the question as to the correctness of them, and as to the wisdom, therefore, of continuing to build, or even attempting to talk about, a strategy of mission based upon them.

In our survey thus far of some attempts by what is termed 'Parish Mission' to bridge the gap between the church and the poor, it will have been observed that one or two common features — we should perhaps say developments — have begun to emerge. For a start, we have found ourselves talking about the church and the world as well as about the church and the poor; and we have been observing the importance attached to two words which have almost become slogans of the church in the post-war period: 'community' and 'laity'. I think these are both encouraging signs. If by laity is meant not simply 'the whole people of God' gathered *as* the people of God, but the people of God dispersed in the world, then we are obviously talking about the church in a much more recognisable way, as far as the New Testament is concerned, than if we talk, as we used to do, about the church as either the clergy or the hierarchical system (however it may be constructed) or the buildings. The poor clearly have a much better chance of 'being the church' if they can do that in the fullest possible way without necessarily having to have, or to belong to, any of these three things. Equally, if by 'community' is meant not some sort of idealised social or class community — the 'proletariat' or the 'masses' — but solidarity in the sense of a recognition of our belonging together, not just as church members, nor even as Christian denominations, but as human beings in our brokenness and our creatureliness and our need, then again, it seems to me, we are talking about something which is at least within the grasp of the poor — often, in fact, more within the grasp of the poor than within the grasp of the rich, dangerous although such a generalisation may seem. Our increasing talk of the 'world' as well as of the 'poor' is both understandable and helpful; understandable, for we are talking, at the moment, about the parish structure of the church and inevitably this touches on many sections of society, not just the poor — some would say, hardly on the poor at all — and desirable, too, because the world is the focus of God's concern, not the church. Much of the thinking about the mission of the church since the war — I am thinking in particular of the World Council of Churches' study on the Missionary Structure of the Congregation in the 1960s — concentrated in particular on the importance of the 'world', especially in the Biblical doctrine of 'creation'. Thus Colin Williams in his book *Where in the World*[12] says 'God speaks, it is assumed, not only from the past in the history of redemption and in the present through the religious life of the church; He also speaks from the world. This speaking from the world — attested to in Scripture in the long line of pagan witnesses — requires the church to have its ears attuned outwards to hear what God is saying from the world, and its eyes focused on the world to see where God is calling us to co-operate with what He is doing in His creation'. This relationship between the church and the world is one to which we must pay increasing attention. Expressed in the formula 'God — World — Church', rather than in the formula 'God — Church — World', to indicate the priority God gives to the world in His mission, the concern for the world, and for taking the world seriously (although not necessarily on its own terms) will introduce into our vocabulary, as it already has introduced into the church's vocabulary, such words as 'dialogue', 'secularisation', 'politics', and 'liberation', to name but four.

Before we move on to look at some attempts to bridge the gap between the church and the poor which have started, as it were, either from the other side of the chasm — from the poor, rather than from the church — or have at least tried to plant one foot on each side and see what sort of bridge then appeared, it will be helpful, now, to mention briefly two movements within the Scottish scene since the war which have played an important part in assembling the materials for building the bridge; I am referring to the Tell Scotland Movement and the work of Industrial Mission.

The building materials

The *Tell Scotland Movement* arose in the 1950s, partly out of the experience of Tom Allan and D P Thomson and others in seeking to mobilise the congregations of the parishes of Scotland for mission, and partly out of the conviction of bodies like the Iona Community and the then Home Board of the Church of Scotland, that mission was directed towards the whole person in the whole world by the whole church. Although it stressed it was a movement and not an organisation, and a movement under the auspices of all the main Protestant Scottish Churches, it nevertheless had a staff, and an organisational structure, and some clearly defined principles. Evangelism, it saw, was the job of the whole church and not just some selected, or even self-selected individuals and groups. It saw evangelism as a constant and not an occasional activity; and the church itself, as the Body of Christ, as the agent of His mission. It saw the church as both something local and something universal. 'Jesus is not only the Light of the lonely heart, He is the Light of the world'. It saw the role of the laity as crucial: the front-line troops in the advance of the church's mission in the world. At the height of its activities in Scotland, Tell Scotland had both a Field Organiser, orientated primarily to mobilising the local congregations for mission in a variety of ways and through a variety of existing groups and organisations, and also a Secretary for the Laity, seeking to develop and build up a strategy of renewal in the localised, secular world. It organised large-scale events, moulded to a large extent on the German *Kirchentag*, called Kirk Weeks; and it had, as well as a number of excellent publications, study groups, or commissions, chaired by such influential figures as Robert Mackie, Ian Fraser, and Murdo Ewan Macdonald, on Evangelism, The Bible, The Laity, and The Community.

There can be no doubt that the church, and the country, as a whole owes a very great deal to the Tell Scotland Movement. My generation within the church was the one most affected by the work, for instance, of the Tell Scotland student teams — groups working at local congregational and parish mission during the university vacations. The Kirk Weeks — there were four in all — powerfully emphasised the fact that the church *is* the people. As Colin Day, the organiser of these Kirk Weeks, has written[13]:

'The church *is* the people, already in the world. I for one never subscribed to the notion that the church, the people, should go out into the world . . . they already *are* there *as* the church and have to function as the Body of Christ within the world from which we can never be extracted until the day of our passing! . . . . I have met people who recalled the Kirk Weeks as life-changing and world-orientating, and they could tell me exactly why.'

As might be expected, however, the orientation of the Tell Scotland Movement in its work amongst the congregations of the Scottish churches was more towards the doing of the old things better than towards the doing of any new thing. In Colin Day's judgment again, there was 'a strong emphasis on "getting the people to church"'; and although undoubtedly the work among congregations was effective in many ways, stimulating much activity and a deal of thought, Tell Scotland, neither in its congregational work, nor even in the Kirk Weeks, made much impact on bridging the gap between the church and the poor. One is tempted to wonder if a humbler title might have helped; the church, after all, has been 'telling Scotland' for many centuries, and one legitimate complaint was that a little more listening and a little less telling might have helped. That said, there can be no denying that Tell Scotland helped, if one may put it thus, in assembling some useful materials in the minds and experience of a number of people and groups, so that further, but very different, attempts to bridge the gap might be tried.

Industrial Mission in this country is a lively and creative force for the Gospel, operating on a UK-wide basis, and deserving of much fuller treatment than we can give it here. There are books and papers on its work, the most interesting of them being those written by Industrial Missioners themselves. However, it would be wrong not to mention it, no matter how inadequately, at this point; for it, too, has played its part in the attempt to bridge the gap between the church and the poor.

Its remit is to Industry — and therefore primarily to those who are in paid employment. For the most part, therefore, Industrial Mission is engaged with those who would not fall into the category of 'the poor' as used in this discussion; although presumably it would have to work with those on the margins of poverty, and it would have a clearer understanding of what I have called 'the story of the poor' than perhaps the normal congregation-based churches would have, being closer to the class to which the poor see themselves as belonging.

Furthermore, Industrial Mission's concern is with working people within the structures of industry, not in order that indigenous groups of Christians should appear on the shop floor and in the board rooms, but in order that there should be a 'reordering of the relationships, methods and goals of industry and commerce in the light of the Christian hope for justice and community and through the process of participation, reflection and evaluation'. To seek to achieve these aims, within the secular, competitive, and often confrontational world of industry and commerce today is a task of some magnitude, and it would be unfair to try to make Industrial Mission responsible for succeeding where the congregational pattern of the church has failed.

Industrial Mission would claim some important areas of advance, nonetheless. It would claim, for instance, that it has played a key role in raising the awareness, within the church and also within the secular world, of the connections between faith, work and politics, and in improving the use of dialogue between church people and work people, especially trade unionists. Industrial Mission has certainly succeeded in bringing before both the church and the world issues of justice, right relationships, and peace — the sort of issues that are to be found in the concept of the Kingdom of God which we saw as belonging essentially to the faith of the church when it first began. These are all areas of advance which cannot fail to be of assistance to the bridging of the gap between the church and the poor. Not that they have been won, at least in some cases, without a great deal of heart-searching and indeed opposition from some quarters–not least from parts of the church itself. As Hugh Ormiston, Industrial Missioner for the Forth Valley, writes[14]: 'Industrial Mission has pushed out the frontiers of church concern into the secular world in a way which, at times, frightens the membership of the churches'. However, in Tom Allan's words, 'for the Church, as for the individual, the point of conflict is the point of growth'.[15]

In these last chapters we have looked at Parish Mission attempts to bridge the gap between the church and the poor, and related movements like Tell Scotland and Industrial Mission, recognising that it is in this area of its missionary outreach and activity that the church has committed by far the majority of its not inconsiderable resources, not just in money, man- and woman-power, and plant, but also in its thinking, its writing and its strategy. I have chosen to do this, who myself am a Parish Minister, with full responsibility, within my own denomination, for sharing in all this activity in every aspect of its thrust, and also with full responsibility for whatever failures it may have had. Some of these attempts — and I have obviously done no more than to try to indicate what I believe are some of the seminal ones, on which many others have been and still are being modelled — have been imaginative, energetic, and not without impressive results, both within the congregations involved and also outside in the life of the world and of the poor.

However, the gap has not been bridged by this method. It has not been bridged, because the attempt, when it has been made, has been started firmly from one side, the side of the church. There is, increasingly perhaps, an awareness of some of the materials that are needed to build the bridge — taking the world seriously, engaging in dialogue, being open to secular concerns, the importance of community and the laity, and so on. Still, the invitation is to the poor to come across the gap themselves, without seeing it from their angle, without really showing them either why they should come across, or even making it possible for them, on the whole, to do so.

Of course there are some poor people in the congregations of our churches, and I have no wish to suggest that the Spirit is not able to use the congregational structures of our churches for His purpose, even among the poor. However, when all is said and done, I am still left with the conclusion that the congregational structure, as an instrument of mission for God to use in His determination to bring in the Kingdom of God amongst the poor, is too blunt an instrument to be able to do it all on its own. As it still is, its ordering is too static, too conservative, too intimate and too parochial for mission today amongst the poor.

Order
Dr E Schwiezer, in his book *Church Order in the New Testament*[16], has drawn our attention to the fact the New Testament word for 'to order' (*tasso*) comes from military terminology and was used to indicate the swift deployment of an army from a marching to a battle formation. This is not the characteristic mark of the church amongst the poor in Scotland today. Indeed, it has been argued, I think convincingly, that the very marks of the church we have inherited from the sixteenth century reformation are just not geared to mission; indeed, that Luther and Calvin believed that the missionary era was over. The church is not geared to being a 'pilgrim people', however powerfully that view may be held and proclaimed from the pulpit. As one Commissioner to a recent General Assembly of the Church of Scotland put it: 'the elders of the Kirk are seen as the pillars of the Kirk, when, in fact, what the Kirk needs are not pillars, but propellers'. We may claim, as the

national church, to be essentially a church of the people, and to be a church of the whole nation (though I pass over here any discussion about whether the church could, in any case, ever be seriously meant to be 'democratic' or whether we should, today, speak about 'national' churches at all). But the fact remains, however uncomfortable it may be felt to be, that we are a clerically-dominated church, still glued to the social world and secular values of our middle-class base, a base which, itself, is beginning to crumble and fall away. Can we start then from the other side? Some have — and in the next chapter we shall examine some such attempts in France, America and Scotland. But I end this chapter with these words from an American source, quoted in Robinson's book *The New Reformation?*[17], which seeks to draw the distinction between 'experiment' and 'exploration' in the mission of the church. The writer refers to 'ministries', but what he says can apply to the full resources of the church, if the church were willing to see it thus:

'*Experimental* ministries, with all their variations, share one assumption that the essential *form* of Christian mission and ministry is known. All presuppose some kind of congregation . . . Many of the activities may take place apart from this gathering and may involve other than members; but the congregation is the center about which all aspects of the experiment revolve. An *exploratory* ministry, on the other hand, presupposes no forms at all. The exploration is entered into precisely because those who undertake it do not presume to know in advance what the structures appropriate to ministry in the urban-industrial culture may be. They set out to explore the metropolitan complex (for example) as objectively as possible, seeking any evidence of ministry actually being performed there, prepared to acknowledge free and responsible servanthood in whatever form it may be found . . . .

The danger to every exploratory ministry is that it will be pre-empted by the institution's demand for structure and "results". "How many new church members has this activity produced?" is not just a crass caricature of the official attitude; it is the question that gnaws at us all from within. We who are involved in exploration sympathise with the poor soul who wrote:

"I wish that my room had a floor.
I don't so much care for a door;
    But this crawling around
    Without touching the ground
Is getting to be quite a bore."

Yet we know, at the same time, that the floor is *there*, and that the way to find it is not to pass prematurely through the door to experimentation . . . .'

References
1 Allan (1954).
2 Garbett (1952), p55f.
3 Allan (1954), p26.
4 Allan (1954), p33.
5 Allan (1954), p44.
6 Allan (1954), p82.
7 Michonneau (1949), p5.
8 Allan (1954), p58.
9 Southcott (1956), p80.
10 Southcott (1956), p17f.
11 Southcott (1956), pp70–74.
12 Williams (1963), p94.
13 In a private letter to the author.
14 In a private letter.
15 Allan (1954), p65.
16 Schwiezer (1961).
17 Robinson (1965), p97.

VI

The exploring church

Secularism/secularisation

In earlier chapters, in particular in Chapter Three, the reader will have noticed that in describing the gap that yawns between the church and the poor, and the various features of the life of the poor over the last century or so in this country, I have not used the words 'secularism' or 'secularisation'. I wish to introduce them at this point, however; not because their use would have been inappropriate before now — in a sense, it could have been a starting point for the whole discussion — but rather because, within the method that I am using, to have entered into an examination of them at an earlier point would have been to run the risk of getting bogged down in concepts and arguments far removed from the felt and shared experience and concerns of both the church and the poor.

Ralph Morton and Mark Gibbs,[1] in their book *God's Lively People*, published in 1971 as a follow-up to their first book, *God's Frozen People*, attempt in Chapter Two to describe what the secular world is like. Their description is not by any means the last word on the subject, or the fullest, for there are other ways of looking at it, such as the ones adopted by Alasdair McIntyre in his Riddell Lectures, published in 1967 as *Secularisation and Moral Change*[2], and in F R Barry's book published in 1969 entitled *Secular and Supernatural*[3] which will repay reading. However, Morton and Gibbs' description will help us here, for we are not about to analyse secularism and secularisation in any great depth, but merely to try to see how what has happened since perhaps 1914 has affected both the church and the poor in the West.

They discern, in the secular world, four main characteristics. First the world is now perceived as *one* world, rather than as a series of isolated worlds such as The Ancient World, The Christian World, The World of Islam, and so on; we can see it as a unity, even photograph it from space — it is a small, known unit that we are speaking of — Planet Earth. Second, it is an *open* world, or better an *interdependent* world; we cannot comfortably and with little concern for our planetary neighbours' needs, or ideas, or life-styles, sit in doubtful security any longer behind our barriers of nation, race, ideology or even religion — much as we far too often desperately try still to do. Third, it is a rather *uniform* sort of world we now find ourselves living in; with our architecture, our technology, our culture, our air travel, we are finding ourselves looking at mirror-images of ourselves all over the place, an experience which we actually do not like as much as we perhaps thought we would, but which is nevertheless real for all that. The fourth characteristic of the secular world of today is what Morton and Gibbs call

> 'a new and fearful sense of our own power and our own responsibility. . . . We can do the most appalling and the most wonderful things to and for each other now; we can, if we wish, deal with problems that have stalked mankind for centuries; we may not hide, any longer, behind the comforting security of the child who trusts that some adult will come along and sort out her problems for her; we have, in that sense, come of age'[4]

To describe the secular world in this way — or indeed in other ways — is not by the same token either to approve or to disapprove of it; it is simply to describe it. Christian reflection on the meaning and significance of it, however, is a different thing. There have been, of course, many such reflections, and it is not my purpose here, even if I were able to, to review them. I would, however, like to make one or two observations which I hope are relevant to our subject.

First, I find myself in the company of those who are inclined to the view that in much of what has happened to the world in this way over the last 70 years or so, we may discern the hand of God. Thus, to return to the description of it given above, I cannot help but feel that it fits in with God's plan for our world that we are able now to see it as one, that we are able to see it now as open and interdependent, and that we are no longer able to act irresponsibly as far as the use of power is concerned — or at least, not without being aware that we do so. How far Christianity, and the Church, have contributed to the appearance of these characteristics, and how far they have sought — and sometimes seem still to seek — to hold them back or even to deny their very existence, I do not propose to discuss; for the record, and on balance, I hold the view that the odds are slightly in the Church's favour. My point, however, is that I am not unhappy about the secular view of the world which we now hold, and I do not feel any need to fight against it. It is there; I am part of it; and I believe it is, on the whole, in accordance with God's design for His world.

None of which, however, is meant to say either that we therefore now know how best to live in this world, or that we no longer need God to help us. That Christendom, and with it the old triumphalist attitude of the church, now no longer can survive in the secular world is for me, as for many, a cause of immense relief; what to Matthew Arnold sounded like the

'melancholy, long withdrawing roar [of the] sea of faith, retreating to the breath of the night-wind down the vast edges drear and naked shingles of the world'

does not sound melancholy to me. However, let us not be under any misapprehension that because we now perceive the world in a secular way, the world has now become in some miraculous sense (if that is the appropriate word) either neutral, or even benevolent and good. As Professor Allan Galloway, in a previous course of Kerr Lectures delivered in the University of Glasgow in 1966, has said: 'it is of the utmost importance that it be clearly understood that there is a secular paganism as well' as a secular Christianity. He goes on, very helpfully, to differentiate between the two:

'the essential difference between Christian secularity and mere secularism is that Christianity acknowledges the confronting presence of God within this "saeculum" — within this age — and sees all culture as a place of responsible meeting with Him. This mode of faith must be sharply distinguished from that of a man who is merely secular — who poses his questions in such a way that he sees only the face of his own culture reflected in a mirror and goes away not knowing what manner of man he is'.[5]

Which brings me to the subject, once again, of the church and the poor. I have suggested earlier that when we describe the situation of the poor in Scotland today, we must highlight certain undeniable features. Thus, we must see it as a tough, rough world; a world containing, in Professor Donnison's angry, emotive words, 'fear, depression, deference, jealousy and supercilious comment'[6]; a world held together also by a consciousness of class solidarity, which includes good neighbourliness and immense unselfishness and self-sacrifice as well as a history of selfishness and sin; a world built on a story of exploitation, struggle, defeat and victory; a world in which the church, and formal religion, is rarely seen as terribly relevant, and even more rarely as an ally. To these features must now be added the following; it is a secular world, in some, but not all, of the senses used in the description of Morton and Gibbs given above; and it is a world in which secular materialism exists awkwardly alongside superstition and a residual folk-religion, a world in which the sense of the reality of God and of costly commitment to His Kingdom (even if it is not recognised as His) marches cheek by jowl with a sense of emptiness, fatalism and despair. It is a world, in other words, in which secular paganism co-exists with both religious and secular Christianity, and these at a variety of levels; a highly complicated and confusing world, in fact, to seek to enter, especially if you seek to enter it from the more ordered world of the church, however secular or religious your experience of the church has happened to be.

Nevertheless, just such an entry has been attempted on a number of occasions in recent times by representatives of the church, concerned to take part in what we have previously identified as 'exploratory' ministries, as against 'experimental' ones — even although they have themselves at times confused the two terms. We shall now look at three of them; they are the Worker-Priest movement in Germany and France in the 1940s and early 1950s; the East Harlem Protestant Parish in New York City in the same period and on into the 1960s; and the Gorbals Group Ministry experiment in Glasgow, of which I was a part, in the 1960s and early 1970s. I shall describe them, even if only in outline; compare and contrast them; evaluate them in a tentative way; and ask what they have to offer to us today as we seek to find a way of bridging the gap between the church and the poor.

Worker-Priest movement
The story of the Worker-Priest Movement in Germany and France, running from the last years of the Second World War through to the first part of the 1950s is available for English-speaking readers in books like *Priest-Workman in Germany*[7] by one of the first of them, Henri Perrin, and in a symposium on the Movement edited by David L Edwards in 1961[8].

The story begins with the Archbishop of Paris, Cardinal

Suhard, and the formation before the war of the JOCIST movement — the Young Catholic Workers. Regarded as — and indeed
actually called — 'militants' by the hierarchy, these young men
and women, under the enthusiastic leadership of young priests,
saw themselves as the spearhead of a new movement of the Spirit
within both the Roman Catholic Church in France and within the
de-Christianised masses of the French city slums. Seeing themselves very much as the leaven in the lump, they organised
themselves into small cells, firmly disciplined, and committed
themselves to a life of study, and of action and witness, based on
the 'see-judge-act' principle which was later to inform bodies such
as the Iona Community and the Christian Workers League in
Scotland.

After France and Germany signed the Armistice in 1941, a new
situation arose, with thousands of French workers being trans-
ferred to Germany, either as forced labour or on a voluntary basis,
to work in the munition factories and industrial complexes of the
Fatherland, in support of the war effort of the Axis powers. Some
of the young priests attached to the JOCIST movement decided,
with the Cardinal's blessing, to go with them; voluntarily to
disguise their priesthood, taking off their soutanes and training as
workmen before they went, in order to share their lives with the
exiled French workers, and there, in Germany, to seek to begin
what Perrin saw as the start of the reconquest of France for the
Gospel and the church.

The details of their experience in Germany need not delay us
here; in Perrin's autobiographical account of the few months he
was able to remain there, active and undetected by the Gestapo,
until he was discovered, imprisoned and finally expelled, the
reader will find a most thrilling account of Christian discipleship
in the modern world. With the war over, the young men who had
undergone this sort of experience were quite sure of one thing:
that the way to win back the masses for Christ in France was not to
return to the old way, to the soutane and the priests' house and the
institutional church, but rather to remain where they had been
forced to place themselves in Germany during the war, with the
masses, as workmen, but also as priests.

The task confronting them was daunting in the extreme. The
world they sought to live in so completely was, in the words of one
of them, 'a neglected, frustrated, rejected world, a world which
had organised itself by its own efforts . . . yet . . . a world where the

power of God is to be shown, where religion is present although it has not yet taken a form visible to human eyes . . . a world in which the Church lives although in theory she is denied any place at all'.[9] Their purpose was 'not to bring the working class back to the Church, nor to make room for it within the old institution; it was that the Church should live in this new world coming to birth, a world in which the poor and the exploited should assume the role of responsible producers.'[10] As Catholic priests, of course, they both saw themselves, and were seen, when recognised, as the focus around which the church, however it might come to be, would have to grow; but any temptation to dictate the nature of that growth, if they felt it at all, was very quickly knocked out of them by the pressure of their lives. Listen again to the reflection of one of them on their experiences:

> 'Silence and withdrawal became a necessary phase of their lives, like the seed of corn hidden in the earth. Deeper still, the pressure of events made them become double men, belonging to the world of faith through their vocation and to the sceptical world through their daily lives. They were not in between these worlds, harassed by doubts; they *belonged* to both. In the world of faith, as it was organised, they knew that the aspirations of the world in which they lived had no place and were not recognised. In the world of unbelief they were ignorant, even if they did not always admit it to themselves, of the meaning that their message could have: in more precise terms, what version of it would be intelligible to the working-class mind. A new religious language had to be created to replace the one which was now for our contemporaries no more than a dead language, like Latin and Greek, and it was not enough to modernise a few scholastic or biblical quotations, as theologians speak Latin with a French pronunciation. An uncomfortable see-saw position which did not make it any easier for them to explain things!'[11]

In spite of these profound tensions, however, there can be no question but that the Worker-Priests involved themselves, up to the hilt, in the world they sought to win.

> 'Ninety-five per cent of them were members of the Trade Union Movement; they took part in strikes, and some of them led large-scale ones; they were involved in numerous rows; two of them got their faces smashed; they were militants in the Peace Movement or other working-class organisations; they fought for the social, political and spiritual emancipation of a class of men, shoulder to shoulder with the communists'.[12]

They never doubted but that their Christian duty was to become involved in class struggle, accepting the class war 'as a fact like gravity which must therefore be taken into account, one of the factors of life, and therefore of action'; and in all this they were sustained by their faith.

> 'If the proletariat is to express itself and really live in a Catholic, universal church alive to its problems, then we, its priests, had to learn its life by living it. It was not just for fun, nor because we were told to, that we did this. It was in sober truth, and driven by the Spirit of God, that we repeated as we contemplated His face and His commands: "He became flesh, in everything like unto men."'[13]

By the mid 1950s, the Vatican and the Roman Catholic hierarchy had ended the Movement and the Worker-Priests had been suppressed. The immediate causes for this decisive action by the hierarchy are not hard to seek. They openly sided with one class; they worked alongside militant Communists for justice and peace; they became victims of their own success, being accused of developing a cult of personality; it was felt that they were in danger of being led by the nose by political activists, not being discriminating enough in their political activities; above all, they were seen as a lay movement. They saw it, naturally, from a slightly different angle:

> 'We are rejected, as the working class is rejected, by the established order, on account of our active participation in the labour struggle, and because the church, through the majority of her members and institutions, defends a regime against which we fight alongside the working class with all our might, because it is oppressive and unjust'.[14]

However, with the advantage of hindsight, it becomes very clear that the hierarchy in fact suppressed them because they put a question to the church, even just by their very presence, which the church did not know how to answer. What are you going to do about the world of the de-Christianised masses, they demanded — if not this, then what? In previous centuries, the Roman Catholic Church had often been able to cope with members who posed awkward questions by turning them into religious orders, and so institutionalising them eventually. However, they could not do this with the Worker-Priests, so firmly rooted and grounded were they in the real, secular, political world. That, of course, was the real problem; the problem was not the existence of the Worker-Priests, but the existence of the world in which they lived.

They lived in it, remember, not as experimenters, but as explorers; as explorers who were also Roman Catholic priests, with their high view of the church, the priesthood and the sacraments. They were not Reformed ministers, instinctively looking for a community to form around the Bible — we cannot, in fairness, blame them if that, then, did not happen. Ted Wickham has criticised them also for their failure to build up the laity, and has claimed that a similar Movement in Britain would seriously damage the 'first priority of mission appropriate to the British scene and a reformed church, namely the engagement of the church with the world through the laity'.[15] If, by the phrase 'the engagement of the church with the world through the laity', Wickham has in mind the sort of engagement which the Worker-Priests undertook, at such cost to themselves, and if he believes that such can be achieved, with the appropriate training, equipping and sustaining of enough lay people so that serious and deep-seated exploration of the world of the poor can be done, in the face not just of the internal pressures of living in such a way, at the very frontiers, but also of the external pressures of the institutional church, demanding all the time results, models, experiments, church members — then I agree with him. There is little sign that this is even being attempted, let alone achieved in Scotland today.

The Worker-Priests, as explorers, discovered things — and their despatches were not wholly ignored or rejected by the church. Without their voyages of discovery, much of what eventually came through in the Second Vatican Council might never have surfaced at all. The importance of the world and its secular concerns; the real cost of being the church *in* the world but not *of* the world; the church as the people of God, and the pilgrim people of God; these, among others, were the messages that the church received, in time, from the Worker-Priests among others.

Another message, which cannot be put into a decree or a document or a strategy for mission, and one of the remarkable aspects of the whole event of the suppression of the Worker-Priests in the 1950s, was the way most of them remained silent in the face of what must have felt like betrayal by the very hand that fed them. To some, no doubt, this looked like loyalty — indeed, like a very remarkable kind of loyalty — and undoubtedly there was something in that view. However, there was more than that, for when you cut your way out into the world from the church — determined, as far as possible, to live off the land, without taking with you all the paraphernalia of the institution for security, making such progress as you can without the aid of maps because there are none, and discovering all the time that your own internal navigational equipment is almost totally inappropriate for this journey you are making, then you find, also, that there is not a lot you can actually say. There are not a lot of people who are in a position even to understand the few stumbling, awkward things you can say. It is not pride that keeps you silent; it is not even loyalty; you simply do not know what words to use. Your life is your statement; its living, its loving, its suffering, its failure; and almost all you have to keep you going are some water, some bread, some wine and a book.

East Harlem Protestant Parish

While the Worker-Priests were exploring, discovering, suffering, and finally being suppressed in Germany and France, another group of young men and women were engaged in exploration, and also in experimentation, on the other side of the Atlantic, in New York's East Harlem. The story of the East Harlem Protestant Parish has not yet, so far as I know, been written up by anyone who was actually involved in it for any length of time, although important reflections from those involved, on a number of aspects of mission, have appeared. Bruce Kenrick's book *Come Out the Wilderness*[16] gives, however, a powerful flavour of what it was about and what it felt like, and while one obviously recognises that this was written by an outsider looking in, it remains the only available introduction to their work.

In the years immediately following the end of the Second World War, a group of young Protestant ministers and their wives moved in to work in this area, a bulging inner-city slum precinct inhabited mainly by Puerto Ricans and black Americans. The mainline churches had mostly departed, or retained a small, nominal presence, but eventually the East Harlem Protestant Parish came to be supported by seven major Protestant denominations. Starting in a small store-front church with a congregation of one, they saw themselves as 'colonists of heaven', likening themselves to 'swimmers struggling to rescue drowning men — needing to feel the same strong currents, the same threats to existence, yet to be able to point the way to shore where we might together find new life and share in the joy of Christ'. They did not seek to become fully identified with East Harlem or anywhere else for that matter, but rather 'to participate in its life, its suffering and joy, its hopelessness and frustrations'. Like their French counterparts, they sought to immerse themselves in the life of the area without benefit of clergy, becoming involved in social and political struggles for justice, for better housing, for human dignity and against all the intense pressures of slum life, drugs, violence, exploitation, family break-up, financial disaster and personal despair. Starting, however, with a different ecclesiology from that of the Worker-Priests, they paid particular attention to two areas of missionary activity which produced a different, and perhaps for our purposes a more recognisable, result.

First, they bound themselves together by a carefully worked out discipline. This involved: participation in the life of the local congregations as they emerged, however small and tentative they inevitably were; the planning of their day, including devotional discipline in their homes; total commitment to live and to act within the community; weekly Bible study and communion and a monthly day of retreat; shared decision-making; a detailed shared financial discipline; and a commitment to work together in the political life of the area. This discipline served the basic purpose of sustaining them through the early years when they were very much on their own; and, modified not without deep struggle and questioning, opened out to become, in many respects, a discipline for the small local congregations that began to emerge as a result of their presence in the area.

Second, they looked to see emerging — and did in fact see — 'congregations of Christ's people who could be the heart of the Parish.' The parish began in 1948, and by 1952, the one small store-front had become three, each responsible for a street or block; they had received the use of a Presbyterian Church building in the area, and were planning to build another one for themselves. With these small congregations — 'colonies of heaven' — they were recovering, as they saw it, integrity in a number of basic Christian practices: in preaching, through the disciplined use of corporate Bible study, based on a common lectionary, by all the members; in communion, found through being a real family together, in demanding fellowship; and in baptism, found in becoming a community where people were really 'born again', changed, becoming saints in humility and 'for real' in the place where they lived.

They developed institutions within the Parish. Not the recognisable and traditional institutions of the mainline churches; rather, institutions arising out of the real needs of the people of the area, and based on their commitment to reclaim the whole of the Parish for Christ by seeking always, in the words of an observer in 1958, 'to learn as well as to teach, to find new religious depths and values as well as to give religious leadership'. Thus, they established a Narcotics Programme, a Credit Union, and a country holiday centre (Parish Acres) as well as building up worship centres in the store-fronts and church buildings; and they staffed these with highly committed and trained personnel, both from outwith and from within the local community.

The Revd Bill Webber, one of the original group in the Parish, gave, in a paper to the Ecumenical Institute at Bossey in Switzerland in 1958[17] an important assessment of the nature of the authority for their work in East Harlem which is worth examining in a little detail. It is important, he claims, to establish what their authority for evangelism is,

> 'otherwise, one is almost driven, sooner or later, to look for results, to seek signs and tokens of success that the world can see . . . . There is no way out by methods of evangelism or new organisations or anything else we devise . . . . Neither our enthusiasm, nor our bright ideas for social action, nor our moral purity, nor our compassion for the broken-ness of East Harlem were of much avail. Our authority could not be found in human terms. Our dependence is not on our solutions or even on our faithfulness, but upon the faithfulness of God in the miracle of the resurrection'.

Arising from this understanding of their authority, certain things followed. They did not see themselves as intruders into the world of East Harlem — although they recognised very clearly, and struggled constantly against, the temptation of what Webber calls 'cultural intrusion' — the temptation to 'overwhelm or dominate, to cajole or entice, those to be evangelised' and to see things all the time 'through eyes predominantly focussed by middle-class standards and values and not by the Gospel'. In Webber's view, it is already God's world, and man is the intruder, by his disruption of the good work of creation. 'The evangelist therefore does not intrude but rather, in urgency and faith, announces to men what God has done for them'.

Their credentials were not themselves, but the church itself — as Webber says, when Jesus was asked for His credentials, He could only point to His life. So they sought to build up the life of the little churches in the area — a life of deep participation in the world, which gave them the chance of genuine communication; a life of involvement in politics and social concerns, for, again in Webber's words, 'most of the serious social problems could only be confronted in this arena'; and a life of service to neighbour, for 'in service, we earn the right to speak'. These little churches were their credentials, and nothing else — this was all they could offer, to be accepted or rejected by the people of the area. So they paid particular attention to all aspects of the lives of these churches — and especially to the liturgical life, in which they sought, imaginatively and with a fair amount of success, to develop a liturgy which really did express the life of the community, which really was a worthy offering to God of their whole lives, 'warts and all'.

The importance of the East Harlem Protestant Parish for our concern to bridge the gap between the church and the poor lies in a number of aspects. There is, first of all, their understanding of why they were there in the first place — because God was already there, because they had in obedience to witness to Him in humility, in participation, and in service as well as in worship. Like other explorers, they took the world very seriously, and did not go in assuming that they knew either what it was like or what God intended it to become. Second, there is their willingness to pay the price for this openness; a price paid in full, not just in terms of cultural confusion and personal hardship and struggle, but even in physical, and in one case in mortal, terms. They were totally committed to the church, but not to their idea of the church, although they did not doubt some sort of congregation would emerge, doing clearly recognisable things like worshipping on Sundays, celebrating the sacraments, and serving in the world. (Here it may be important for us to consider the searching question posed by the American group already quoted in an earlier chapter, as it appears in John Robinson's book *The New Reformation?*[18]: 'Have we been right in assuming that, still in our time, some form of "fellowship" (*koinonia*) is indispensable to the Christian community? and if so, what does it *look like?*'). Finally, they were forced to face, at the deepest level, the need for discipline, and for corporate discipline as well as personal discipline, and for corporate and personal discipline which did not just cover the normal areas of religious and pious devotion, but which covered the use of time, of money, and of buildings, and controlled areas of life that we have grown so accustomed to regarding as private — like making decisions about jobs and residence, like involvement in politics and so on.

Because, unlike the French Worker-Priests, the East Harlem Protestant Parish was both exploratory and experimental, their ministry has, I think, more actually to say to us, in words and actions that we can understand, even if we cannot immediately see how to follow them. The principles outlined above: following God into the real and total world, refusing to dictate the agenda, being willing to pay the price for obedience, believing in and seeing the emergence of the small local church, and accepting the need for a full corporate and personal discipline in every aspect of their lives; these principles, I suggest, are not ones that can ever be ignored — none of them — if the gap is to be bridged.

Are they adaptable to the Scottish scene? Indeed, are these experiences from the Continent and from America really relevant and practical for Scotland today? The next chapter's description of the work of the Gorbals Group in Glasgow, which moulded itself to a very large extent on aspects of both the experiences outlined in this chapter, may show us that it is possible, but also highly risky and demanding, to do so.

References

1 Morton and Gibbs (1964); Morton and Gibbs (1971).
2 McIntyre (1967).
3 Barry (1969).
4 Morton and Gibbs (1971), pp27–37.
5 Galloway (1967) p47ff.
6 Donnison (1982), p228.
7 Perrin (1947).
8 Edwards (1961).
9 Edwards (1961), p83f.
10 Edwards (1961), p95.
11 Edwards (1961), p90f.
12 Edwards (1961), p45.
13 Edwards (1961), p51.
14 Edwards (1961), p51.
15 Edwards (1961), p146f.
16 Kenrick (1962).
17 Webber, George W. 'A Study on the meaning of Evangelism', unpublished paper.
18 Robinson (1965), p97.

VII

The Gorbals Group ministry

My purpose in this chapter is to examine in some detail the work of the Gorbals Group Ministry in Glasgow in the late 1950s and throughout the 1960s — an exploration which did not quite become an experiment. Of all the attempts to bridge the gap between the church and the poor which we have examined so far, this is the one about which I must be regarded as being most suspect; for our family belonged to this group for eight years, from 1963 to 1971, some of my closest friends were also members of this group and I am still involved with some of them today. Objectivity, therefore, is going to be seriously at risk in what I have to say.

First, let me take you to a regular meeting of the Gorbals Group Ministry as it actually happened in September 1966. Before we begin, I shall attempt a short description of the area as it existed then, based upon a detailed report by the UK-wide organisation, Christian Action, on Gorbals published in 1965.[1]

The location
Gorbals in 1963 comprised two adjacent areas of inner-city tenement housing on the south bank of the River Clyde, called Hutchesontown and Laurieston. They originated at different periods in the city's history, and for different purposes. Hutchesontown, the area to the east of Gorbals, had grown up at the end of the nineteenth century and the beginning of the twentieth, primarily in response to the great influx of immigrants to Glasgow to feed the ever-expanding demand of the city's industrial sector. The tenements contained small apartments — sometimes a single room, sometimes two or even three rooms, mainly with outside toilets — and as they grew, and became packed and more than packed with people from the Highlands, the Lowlands, Ireland and Central Europe, as well as with native Glaswegians, they became known as 'instant slums'. By the middle sixties, however, the end was in sight for the old Hutchesontown; a development

plan had been drawn up as early as 1951, and by 1965 the Corporation of Glasgow, firmly committed to demolishing the old tenements and building high-rise flats and new shopping centres, was slowly moving into action. Tenements were being pulled down; a few new flats (low-rise) had been built; and the internationally renowned architect of Coventry Cathedral, Sir Basil Spence, was 19 months behind schedule with two new high-rise tower blocks of 400 houses being erected on vacant ground.

The subsequent history of Hutchesontown, trumpeted as the first Redevelopment Area in Glasgow, makes disturbing reading, with new low-rise housing developments opened in the early 1970s and closed apparently because of design faults and for other reasons, before the end of that decade. Our concern here, however, is more with the other area, to the West, called Laurieston, for it was here that the Gorbals Group really belonged.

Laurieston appeared earlier than Hutchesontown. David Laurie developed the large flats and spacious streets of Laurieston in place of the late mediaeval weaving burgh of Gorbals, early in the nineteenth century, in the hope that he would attract to his new suburb the *nouveau riche* of Glasgow's growing commercial and business sector. He gave his streets posh-sounding English names: South Portland Street, Norfolk, Cumberland, Carlton Place — and threw in a bit of Walter Scott, in Abbotsford Place, for good measure. The houses he built, tenement-style as always, were nevertheless poles apart from the 'instant slums' of the later Hutchesontown; most flats were of seven spacious rooms, entered from a spiral staircase in a turret running up the back of the building, and bounded on the front with broad elegant streets, and at the back with neat, grass-covered back courts.

The hopes of David Laurie were, however, never quite realised. The *nouveau riche* moved out from the town centre, not south to Laurieston, but West to Kelvinside and Great Western Road; and instead of bankers and lawyers and businessmen, his flats were first populated with teachers, skilled craftsmen, managers, and even ministers. A fascinating study of *The Story of a Street*, compiled by a group from Strathclyde University in the 1960s, surprised everyone by revealing the high proportion of pianos to be found in the homes of South Portland Street in the latter half of the nineteenth century, and also the quite large numbers of maids who found employment there. But by 1965, David Laurie's dream had become a nightmare. The Laurieston area of Gorbals now contained just over 18 000 people. They still lived in Laurie's large flats, by now divided and sub-divided often into accommodation for three, or even four or five families in each flat, but by 1963, the Corporation of Glasgow had declared 63 per cent of these flats unfit for human habitation, and 99 per cent of them to be of the lowest structural category — in the words of the Christian Action report, 'one category before they fall down!' Six hundred and seventy-six families were surveyed in this area by the Christian Action team. One hundred and forty-nine of them had a bath in their homes — 528 had none. In the sub-lets, the average number of people per room was 2.73; this compares with an average for Glasgow as a whole of 1.27, for Edinburgh of 0.94, and for Liverpool of 0.82. In the county town of Cambridge, it was 0.64.

Statistics are helpful, if frightening. To get the feel of the place, however, one has to resort to impressions. This is how the Christian Action team saw Gorbals in 1965[2]:

'Official complacency and guilt is hiding the truth that Gorbals is the worst slum in Britain and is rapidly deteriorating .... The evidence is there in black and grey. It shows on the buildings; once elegant mid-Victorian homes but now decayed memories of their former selves. During the day it is hard to believe that behind the windows in many of these streets is one of the worst overcrowding problems in Europe. The houses would seem to be desolate. Hardly anywhere is there a complete set of window panes and curtains are an exception. At the backs of the houses, and up the stairways, the windows are all broken, leaving gaping holes in the walls, the frames holding sharp pieces of glass on which children can injure themselves. At night the windows are lit by naked light bulbs, sometimes behind flimsy curtains or a piece of cardboard in place of a window pane. The back courts that once had been green lawns protected by iron railings are now infested wastelands, scarred with troughs holding pools of stagnant yellow water. Everywhere there is filth and rubbish, the ally of disease and vermin. The streets are a shambles'.

The Gorbals Group, as they gathered into a first-floor flat in one of these streets on a September evening in 1966, carried with them the experience of living that day in that place — and in other places throughout Glasgow. There were 25 people assembled in the large sitting room for the meal with which every Group meeting began. Five were visitors to the Group that evening. Another was a social work student attached to the Group on placement. There were four voluntary helpers, regularly present but not full members of the Group; twelve full Group members; and, last but by no means least, three local Gorbals people. Of the dozen full members present, six were single people, five married and one a single parent. They all lived within the Laurieston area, all within close proximity of each other — and some had already seen each other at various points throughout the day. Their day's activity reflected the concerns of the Group Ministry. Thus, two of them had been engaged in Nursery School teaching, and two in work with the Glasgow Social Work Department; three had been at home, keeping house and looking after children and a variety of visitors; one had been involved for part of the day in legal work in connection with some housing cases in which the Group had an interest; and four of them had been alongside a variety of individuals and families in the area. For the record, five of them were qualified as professional church workers — four ministers and a deaconess — but only two, the deaconess and a minister, worked within a local congregation, and one other minister received a stipend from the Church, although his work connected with no recognisable church organisation.

A Group meeting

After the meal and a Communion service around the same table, the Group took up the business of the evening. The minutes of that September meeting in 1966 show that the concerns of housing were high on the Group's priorities at that time — hardly surprising when one thinks of the state of the place they were living in. There were other things also on their minds. Three new projects were under review, as things started up again after the summer. There was a proposal to open a cafe, and one of the local Gorbals people present was interested in the possibility of working in it for the Group. The idea of starting up a local newspaper had been floated earlier, and plans were now being made to get down to work and see if this could be produced. A suggested programme of study for the Group was outlined by one of the members. (For the record, the cafe project never got off the ground; the other two did). Other issues were dealt with — the disposal of a billiard table, reports on problems with a building used as a day nursery and on the difficulties of having too many drivers for the Group van, a proposed visit to the area by the Moderator of the General Assembly of the Church of Scotland (but nobody was quite sure *where* he was going to speak!), and a decision to subscribe to the Child Poverty Action Group, (and to appoint an absent Group member as the Group's representative!).

Then, the business over, Evening Prayers. The corporate reading of Luke 4:16–19: 'Jesus came to Nazareth, and He went as His custom was on the sabbath day to the synagogue. He stood up to read. And there was given to Him the book of the prophet Isaiah . . . .' Then a liturgy of intercession for Gorbals:

Let us bring to God the needs of His world, remembering especially the people of this place in their homes, in the streets, and at their work.
We remember...and . . . and . . . .
Lord Christ, we uphold your people
for mercy and for blessing
By your healing of the diseased
   Lord, heal the sick
By your fortitude in the storm
   Lord, calm the fearful
By your fondness for little children
   Lord, protect the young
By your labour at a bench
   Lord hallow your work
By your forgiveness on the cross
   Lord, pardon our sins
By your rising from the dead
   Lord, give us life.

Then out into the streets again — to another night, another day.

The Thursday night Group meeting, of which the one outlined above is fairly typical, had been going ever since the start of the Group in 1958 — and continued until the end, in the early 1970s. In fact, an attempt had been made to start the Group in 1954. Three young Church of Scotland ministers, Geoff Shaw, John Jardine and Walter Fyfe, had pooled their ideas (and in the case of Geoff and Walter, their experience of the East Harlem Protestant Parish) and had proposed a roughly similar scheme for an inner area of Glasgow (not necessarily Gorbals at that point) to the Presbytery of Glasgow. Their idea then (and it did not substantially alter when it was put forward again three years later) was to go and live in one house in the area, with the aim of visiting around the doors, sharing the lives of their neighbours, and seeking to enable a small local congregation to emerge, 'centred on the sacraments, on preaching and on worship', and in time, perhaps, developing 'house-meetings, fellowships and perhaps even pastoral groups'.[3] They had previously done a survey of the institutional church congregations which already existed in the area; but had come to the conclusion that these did not really represent the majority of the Gorbals people, who, in the main, were not present in these buildings on a Sunday. It was 'no for the likes of them'.

New ways

Their initial proposals, which were turned down by the Presbytery in 1954 but accepted three years later, indicate that they saw themselves as going out as explorers for the church into unknown territory. 'We wish to try some new ways to bring a knowledge, so far as we can understand and interpret it, of Christ's person and of His will for individuals and communities, to predominantly pagan districts'.[4] Before they went, they had, however, a rough idea of what they wanted to see happen — as described above, clearly it derives from the East Harlem experience of two of them, although important antecedents can be found also, as they acknowledge, in the Worker-Priest Movement, and in the thinking, for instance of Stephan Neill, at that time an Assistant General Secretary with the World Council of Churches, who had written powerfully on the subject of 'street churches' in the Church of Scotland's magazine *Life and Work* in May, 1954. Geoff Shaw, in a separate paper written at this time, argues that the experiments of Allan and Michonneau are not very helpful for Scotland, as a whole, for their basis is too wide, and their demands too high — for him, as for his colleagues, the very local, very limited, and very low-key approach of East Harlem seemed to offer a better chance of reaching the un-churched people of Gorbals in a more realistic way. Shaw argued: 'We believe the Church of Scotland has the responsibility of choosing in favour of both sides of the dilemma.' (He refers to the dilemma of congregation or parish). The church must 'reach out with the full Gospel now to those furthest away from the church, at the same time as the church prepares her members to fulfil their mission'.[5]

These early policy documents of the Group, written of course before they had actually started, bear inevitably the mark of inexperience and a certain brash idealism, for neither of which it would really be fair to blame them. They reveal also, however, a worrying confusion of the exploratory and the experimental in their approach, which was to have quite serious consequences later on, for it seems as if they wished to have their cake and eat it. They wanted to have the freedom to go out into the pagan world of Gorbals, confident that some form of little churches would spring up round them (and confirmed in this view by East Harlem's experience), but not at all clear what the relationship of these little churches would eventually have to the mainline churches to which the three of them belonged (and not at all clear, either, on how they were going to deal with the denominational divide of Gorbals, between Catholic and Protestant, which was to prove one of the major barriers to the appearance of any such little local congregations). They wanted to be explorers, but along certain well-defined lines; and they wanted to keep in touch with, and have the blessing of, their sending base, the Church of Scotland. When they actually set out on their journey, with the blessing of the church, they found themselves in quite different country from what they had imagined; they found that their own internal equipment, their expectations, and their personal differences produced a very different reaction to what they were finding from what they had thought would result; and they found, too, that they were very rapidly losing touch with base, as the lines of communication quickly began to fail and fade. Without wishing to labour the comparison, they began, as it were, in the company of the East Harlem Protestant Parish, and eventually ended up much more in the company of the French Worker-Priests.

The early minutes of the Group Meetings which in those days numbered first five, and then seven, members — reveal both what they were finding and also the tensions that were developing, some quite creatively, others not so helpfully. From the start, they adopted the disciplines of the East Harlem Protestant Parish; living in the area (first in one common house, then splitting up into four separate homes); pooling all their income and sharing in a common, low, standard of living; sharing decision-making in a very full way; becoming gradually more and more deeply involved in the whole life of the community, socially and politically as well as in other more personal ways; getting to know their neighbours; and meeting weekly for Communion, Bible study, prayer, and discussion on their life and work. The pressures of the place soon began, inevitably, to dominate and to decide their activities: the needs of the children, the housing problems, the necessary move into the arena of party politics, and always people, people, people.

Very quickly they found that they had to allocate certain areas of work to certain members; thus, Geoff Shaw worked with older teenagers, John Jardine worked in a local secondary school and in the whole field of education, Walter Fyfe found his field in the area of politics and industry, and Kirstie Wedderburn and Ray Soper, who joined later, were mainly concerned with younger children. All were, in the words of Walter Fyfe, 'furiously experimenting in their own areas'.[6]

Doubts

But what of their original purpose — 'to provide each small natural community . . . with a centre of worship and to break down the large anonymous area into smaller and more personal groups', with these centres of worship developing congregations which would 'serve this small area, meeting perhaps in homes, perhaps in a disused shop or warehouse, which would not only be a centre of worship but also a family centre for all in the area'?[7] In their report to the local Church of Scotland Presbytery in 1960, it is clear that this was not happening; not only that, but it is evident that they were now far from sure that it ever could — and subsequent discussion shows that, for some of them at least, there was doubt as to whether it even should happen at all. Thus, while John Jardine, by 1960, was worrying about their failure 'to share our shared life with other people in the area', and wondering if this was 'because we are not at all sure that we really believe in the Church'; and while Geoff Shaw was feeling that they were failing to expound 'the basic *kerygma*', and that there was room for improvement in their 'waiting on the Lord'; Walter Fyfe, the most radical of the Group at that point, was rejecting the Church in its entirety, as being the equivalent of 'the old Israel', and was writing: 'Mission, evangelism, must grow out of obedience, which is primary', and 'if nobody sees Christ in, and through us, then He just isn't in us, and it's no use kidding'. Most committed of all to exploration in the fullest sense of the word, Fyfe saw his work as a labourer in industry (while still a minister) as being in order to 'know whether it is possible for a worker to follow Christ', and if any sort of congregation was to evolve within the area, then it must be with no preconceived pattern or structure, but 'ministers, managers, doctors, labourers, Christians and non-Christians must form the group of disciples we are earnestly seeking'.[8]

The Presbytery, understandably, were ambivalent about what

was going on. They encouraged the Group to continue, seeing it thus far as a 'worthwhile experiment' which needed more time to develop, but they felt certain areas needed to be clarified and corrected. Thus, they were worried about the Group's lack of concern to hold services on Sundays; they felt that the emphasis on Communion as the one act of worship they offered, served to exclude children and those in the area not prepared to join in the sacrament; they worried about the undervaluing of preaching; and they felt that the stringent emphasis on financial sharing excluded those who could not join in at that point. These concerns are clearly reflected in the comments of a former member of the East Harlem Protestant Parish, Flossie Borgmann, who was with the Group for a time at this point. She highlights in particular the problem of getting local people involved, especially in view of the denominational differences present in the area; the problem of people attaching themselves to the Group for what they felt they could get out of the Group (shades of Thomas Chalmers here?); the problem of the Group's tight financial discipline turning them into an elite in the area; and the difficulty of attracting men, as against women, into the life and concerns of the Group, especially in an area like Gorbals, which was very much a matriarchial society. 'If the aim of the Group', she writes, 'is to create a new community free from the institutional church and to do this by participation in all sections of life . . . this demands . . . the participation of local people in policy making, and also to share in worship, sacraments, and Christian teaching'.[9]

From 1960 onwards, while these issues continued to exercise the minds of the Group, of visitors to it, and of the Churches in so far as they continued to be related to the Group; it is fair to say that the direction of the Group's activities moved forward in different ways. John and Beryl Jardine and their family, and then later Walter and Elizabeth Fyfe and their family, left; others, including ourselves, joined; and the Group in Gorbals developed into what one outside observer — an American minister on placement with the Group from the Ecumenical Institute at Bossey in Switzerland — could describe as essentially a *diakonia* group, 'seeking to answer man's longing for a "gracious God" by helping him to experience the reality of a "gracious neighbour"'. The internal disciplines remained, although the financial one was subsequently drastically modified in the hope that this would enable others, especially local people, to join — a hope which was fulfilled only to a very limited degree. The reports of the Group to the parent church body throughout the 1960s indicate clearly that the Group rapidly became less and less concerned with internal relationships, and with any attempts at the formation of little congregations in the area, and more and more committed to seeking to meet the needs of the area and its hard-pressed people. In this commitment, the Group undoubtedly achieved a fair degree of success. Their work alongside young people often carried out at tremendous personal cost; their experiments in what was by then coming to be called Community Development, which included such things as street action groups, a community newspaper, an adventure playground, a nursery school, a youth and community association, a holiday scheme, and an adventure camp in the Highlands; their involvement in local and city politics, leading to one of their members, Geoff Shaw, eventually being elected on to Glasgow Corporation as a Councillor for a neighbouring area; their personal casework with and on behalf of their neighbours; their wider action in issues of justice and peace; their co-operation with training agencies in the fields of social and community work: in all these, and in other areas, the Group was exploring and pioneering often for the first time in Scotland.

Geoff Shaw, in particular, continued right through the 1960s to reflect on the relationship of the developing Group to their original vision, and to the institutional church. In 1963, he wrote:

> 'We have found no neat solutions to the problems of the Church's ministry to those who for one reason or another belong to no church. We remain convinced of the need to share to the full in the life of the community in order that we may properly intercede for it, and to attempt to interpret something of the healing ministry of Christ through our concern for the wholeness of the community in which we live'.[10]

A certain degree of rather prim disapproval comes over in his comment in the 1968 Report that 'during the ten years of the Group's existence no one has become a full member of the Church of Scotland and maintained membership over any length of time';[11] the pressure from the church, and from within some members of the Group themselves, was, as we saw in an earlier chapter, always niggling away at the issue of membership of the institutional church as a mark of success or failure.

Shaw went on, in the same 1968 Report, to try to reflect on why the 'church' bit had not worked. He identified three main reasons. First, he saw clearly what Webber, from East Harlem, had warned against — the danger of 'cultural intrusion'; local people felt 'strange' in what was, essentially, a very middle-class, wordy, and activist group of outsiders who would always remain outsiders however much they sought to 'participate' in (as against 'identify with') the life of the area. The denominational divisions of the West of Scotland, already mentioned, proved a second major obstacle; the gulf between Catholic and Protestant (and the majority of the Gorbals population at that time were Catholic, in culture if not in practice) proved an impassable gulf at the point of worship and church membership, so we see it right to stand, as it were, outside the doors of both denominations'. The problem of 'firmly held misconceptions and distortions of Christianity which is the legacy of bad religious education' forced them into a practice of evangelism which they saw as having to be carried out with no preconditions of membership — 'the love, caring, compassion of the Christian community is unconditional'. So, with commendable honesty, Shaw wrote: 'there has been an indecisiveness of the Group in regard to the formation of some form of congregation, and the inevitable sense of failure that the basic faith of most of the members of the Group has not in fact been adequately shared with others outside the church'.[12]

Local congregations

For the three years from 1966 to 1968 when I worked full-time with the Group, my own experience bears out Shaw's comments given above. My main responsibilities for this period were in youth work, political activity, and the setting up and running of the local community newspaper already mentioned. My main interest, however, even then was to see if little local congregations could emerge from within the area. I approached this from different angles. A number of our neighbours were anxious for baptism for their children; so I sought to work with them, all women, in looking at what baptism meant and how it should be based on a broader belonging to a Christian community. They drifted away — no doubt lost, as I was myself, as to what such a broader Christian community might mean if it did not mean the church as they saw it, with its buildings, its Sunday services, and its 'proper' ministers and priests. I sought to gather together a small group of our neighbours around the Bible, in our house, to explore the Scriptures together — other members of the Group had already tried this before — but I recoiled from this attempt in confusion when I discovered, first, that our Catholic neighbours would not come and, second, that our Protestant neighbours interpreted this activity in terms of the Mission Hall and a Mission-Hall-type faith. We tried Sunday services, in the converted warehouse that was our Youth Club at the time, as the Presbytery had asked us to do; none of our neighbours came, partly because as soon as the flag marked 'worship' was raised, the denominational standard was automatically seen to be flying above it, and partly because they were in their beds anyway. At the end of this period, with my thoughts on the matter much more confused than they had been when I started, I became minister of one of the local congregations in the area; and had to live with the mixture of approval and resigned amusement from our neighbours, as they saw me moving out of their reach, as far as the official church was concerned, back into the 'institution'. It was not a comfortable time.

It may be that someone, sometime, will be in a position to make a balanced and complete judgment on the work of the Gorbals Group, and to assess to the full its value for the mission of the Church in Scotland, and in particular for the mission of the Church in Scotland in relation to the poor and the dispossessed of Scotland. Myself, I am too close to it, both in terms of time and in terms of personal involvement, to imagine that I can say that final word.

If we take as our aim, in seeking to bridge the gap between the church and the poor, Cardinal Suhard's fervent vision of 'the church springing up in the midst of the proletarian masses, taking with them their own attitude of mind, their own way of life and their own organisations' then the Gorbals Group cannot be said to have succeeded. David Rice, a black American Baptist minister who lived in our family for a time when we were in Gorbals (and with whom, incidentally, I was laying the breakfast table when the news came over the radio of Martin Luther King's assassination), described the Gorbals Group as 'indeed a kind of leaven to those whom they came in contact with' but went on to say this:

'I feel that if the Group is to be "the church in the area", it must fulfil its three-fold calling (service — gathering — proclamation).

The questions that are left, then are:

a) In what way can we *really* say that the church is present when social work alone is accomplished? Does it really matter that Christian work be a conscious thing both with the doer and the receiver? And how, in this situation, can the receivers also become the doers in the fullest sense of the word?

b) Do the terms "redemption", "conversion", and "salvation" still have any meaning today, in this situation?'[13]

These questions, together with the searching questions posed by the American group quoted previously, as to whether we are right to assume that, 'still in our time, some form of "fellowship" is indispensable to the Christian community, and if so, what does it look like?' — these questions, the Gorbals Group has not, I submit, answered — although it may have helped to pose them, and others, more sharply to the church. Whether the church wants to hear them, let alone try to answer them, is another matter; I was always sadly disappointed that, with one exception, the Church of Scotland Divinity Halls, for example, never thought fit to send any of their students to be with us the whole time we were there, if for no other purpose than to struggle a bit with some of these questions. The Episcopal Church showed much more interest at this level — as did the World Church.

For a deeper description of the life of one of the members of the Gorbals Group, I recommend the book by Ron Ferguson, simply entitled *Geoff*[14], in which he tells in lively, and very perceptive, form, the story of the life of Geoff Shaw. For myself, I must leave the subject of the Gorbals Group, in the end, on a personal note. I see in my mind's eye the streets of Gorbals, 'shambolic' as always, at night — and Geoff wearily striding round them, following from pub to pub a 14-year-old boy, high on drink and drugs, and saying to me, in a quiet, tired voice: 'You don't have to like them, John — but you have to love them'. I hear a woman saying, of one of the members of the Group: 'She teaches you the right way of doing things, but you don't feel you're being taught'. And I hear the voice of one of our Club boys, delivering his judgment on the area: 'Aye, it's a dump — but it's a good dump'.

References

1 Christian Action (1965).
2 Christian Action (1965).
3 Gorbals Group (1954), unpublished papers.

4 Gorbals Group (1954), unpublished papers.
5 Gorbals Group (c.1954), unpublished papers.
6 Gorbals Group (c.1960), unpublished papers.
7 Gorbals Group (c.1958), unpublished papers.
8 Gorbals Group (1960), unpublished papers.
9 Gorbals Group (c.1960), unpublished papers.
10 Gorbals Group (1963), Report to Glasgow Presbytery.
11 Gorbals Group (1968), Report to Church of Scotland Home Board.
12 Gorbals Group (1968), Report to Church of Scotland Home Board.
13 Private Report to the Gorbals Group (c.1968).
14 Ferguson (1979).

VIII

Good news to the Poor

'Make them my disciples'
Of the two commissioning statements made by Jesus to His disciples, as recorded in the Gospels, the one we are most accustomed to hearing is the one reported as having been made after the Resurrection: 'Go, then, to all people everywhere and make them my disciples; baptise them in the name of the Father, the Son and the Holy Spirit, and teach them to obey everything I have commanded you. And I will be with you always, to the end of the age'. (Matt. 28:19-20) The value of this statement to the church is obvious. It sets before us the larger vision of the whole world won for Christ; it is linked firmly to the sort of church we know, a Trinitarian church, and a baptising church, and above all, a teaching church; and it carries with it an inner strength and confidence, in the promise of Christ's presence 'always, to the end of the age'.

I wonder, however, whether it is the statement we ought to be listening to any longer — at least 'we' who are the rich, the together, the organised, and most of all the Northern, first-world church of today. Of far greater importance to us, I believe, is the other commissioning statement, recorded in its fullest and most powerful version in Matthew 10:5-42. Luke gives, along with Mark, the shorter version: 'Then Jesus sent them out to preach the Kingdom of God and to heal the sick, after saying to them, "Take nothing with you for the journey: no stick, no beggar's bag, no food, no money, not even an extra shirt. Wherever you are welcomed, stay in the same house until you leave that town; wherever people don't welcome you, leave that town and shake the dust off your feet as a warning to them"'. The whole sense of this statement, its foundation in the proclamation of the Kingdom, its commitment to healing and wholeness, its acceptance of poverty, of risk, of rejection, and of confrontation (all of which are powerfully amplified by Matthew) speaks to our time in a way which the first statement completely fails to do.

In the last two chapters we have been considering the activities of disciples to whom the second statement would have made much more sense than the first. The French Worker-Priests, the members of the East Harlem Protestant Parish, and the members of the Gorbals Group, were men and women who saw themselves very much as the sort of disciples described in what is commonly called The Commissioning of the Twelve. They were, as we have already said, essentially explorers; and although some of them, some of the time, crossed the admittedly ill-defined boundary between exploration and experimentation, it is as explorers that they are of most use to us, as we seek to learn from them how to bridge the gap between the church and the poor. Let us try to examine some of their discoveries, which are not so much new, unheard-of finds, but rather rediscoveries of principles and practices which the church, in forgetting or diluting, ignores at its peril indeed.

For a start, they show us, clearly, that to be *in* the world of the poor today, means a depth of participation and commitment which is costly, risky, and fraught with misunderstandings and possibilities of rejection from every angle — including from within. Gustavo Gutierrez, the Latin American 'liberation theologian', puts it this way:[1]

'In recent years it has seemed more and more clear to many Christians that, if the church wishes to be faithful to the God of Jesus Christ, it must become aware of itself from underneath, from among the poor of this world, the exploited classes, despised ethnic groups, and marginalised cultures. It must descend into the hell of this world, into communion with the misery, injustice, struggles and hopes of the wretched of the earth — for of such is the kingdom of heaven! To be born, to be reborn, as church, from below, from among them, today means to die, in a concrete history of oppression and complicity with oppression. In this ecclesiological approach, which takes up one of the central themes of the Bible, Christ is seen as the Poor One, identified with the oppressed and plundered of the world'.

Lost explorers

To enter into the world of the poor in that way is no joke, as I hope has been made clear in the previous two chapters. As we shall see in a moment, it leads one to ask the most searching and fundamental questions about the nature of the church and what it is for — and the answers one keeps coming up with make it extremely difficult to keep one's balance both in today's world and in today's church. If, at various times, some of the explorers we have been looking at have lost their balance — and I include myself in that category — attention should be directed, perhaps not so much to the unbalanced explorer as to the nature of the tightrope he or she was trying to walk in the first place — and the gap over which it was thrown.

To walk it at all — to live in that world — requires, as we have seen, a discipline and a determination of the most practical and effective kind — which will produce, not so much the shock troops of a Society of Jesus, as the clowns of a Society of St Francis. Abbé Godin, speaking of his own and other's attempts to penetrate the world of the pagan masses of the French proletariat after the war, says: 'The Good News must find its incarnation in their human actuality, but this demands first a deeply honest attempt to understand their world, followed by various approaches, many of them tentative'.[2] To make tentative approaches, when the whole ethos of the church in mission is towards certainty, authority, and completeness, requires discipline indeed — and a certain humility which settles for a little, and not the lot. Godin again: 'Christ tells us to ask for our *daily* bread, not for three months' rations! If He gives us light enough to set out by, need we demand to have the whole road floodlit?'[3] Or, in words used often within the Iona Community, 'follow the light you see, and pray for more light'.

I am convinced, however, of the desperate need for more explorations of this kind, if the Kingdom of God is to be truly preached as good news to the poor. Tentative approaches, without stick, bag, food, money or even a spare shirt, are what we need; not great programmes for renewal or projects for mission which fail to start where people are, but are really more efficient attempts to impose alien patterns, however attractively gift-wrapped and renovated, upon 'the poor'. As Ian Fraser, in his book *The Fire Runs*[4] constantly warns us, these tentative approaches will bring in their wake much confusion and uncertainty. 'But may not confusion, disorientation, an unknown future, be gifts of God? May it not be a blessing of God to be brought up sharp, prevented from making any progress, forced back on one's heels, or on one's knees?' Further on in the same chapter, he spells this out again in more detail: 'Whatever is available in comprehensible words is undisturbing to the foundations of thought. It leaves one with one's existing vocabulary and experience intact, and with the overmastering temptation to fit new things into these. What is now needed is a new hearing, new eyes, a new understanding. One cannot edge forward into radically different attitudes. Shock is needed: rupture'.

Perhaps the greatest shock which these and other explorations into the world of the poor administer, first to the explorers and then, perhaps, to the main body of the Church, is that we simply do not know what to do — and we begin not to know who or what we are. In the words of Julio de Santa Ana, 'The Church does not recognise itself in the poor, and the poor do not recognise Christ in the Church'. The pain, bewilderment and confusion of this sort of shock is sometimes more than can be borne — which is why, I imagine, very few people or groups within the church take the risk of exposing themselves to it. Here I would like to refer again to our own experience in Govan a few years ago, after we had conducted our Parish Profile exercise which I spoke about in the first chapter. We held a follow-up Elders' Conference, to examine the Profile in some detail and to try to see what action should result. For me, and I know for others, the most effective result of that conference was not in any programme for action which came out of it — in fact, no great programme for action *did* come out of it; it was rather in the stunned silence around the middle of the third session when, having looked in detail at the sort of people and their life-style who actually did live round our church door, someone asked, 'What would happen if these people did actually come into the church?'. In truth, I now think we should have stopped the conference at that point, for in the pain and the confusion and the guilt and the defensiveness of that silence there were probably at the same time more seeds of hope for the future than in any of the stumbling words and ideas that we went on to toss around, to console ourselves with.

But let there be no mistake here; I am not simply advocating exploration and listening and silence and participation and discipline and humility and even disorientation and confusion because all these things are, somehow 'good' for the church; still less am I advocating them in order that the existing church in Scotland, suitably humbled and chastened and restored, can then set about 'doing the job better the next time'. The challenge of the Latin American theologians is at its sharpest here which is why, I imagine, it is at this point that their words are most hotly disputed by the church in this country. De Santa Ana says: 'The Church which is not the Church of the poor puts in serious jeopardy its churchly character'[5] and, Sobrino puts it even more bluntly: 'In principle a Church *for* the poor is not yet a Church *of* the poor. . . . The Church of the poor is not a Church for the poor but a Church that must be formed on the basis of the poor and that must find in them the principle of its structure, organisation, and mission'.[6]

Urban Priority Areas

It is virtually impossible to imagine that any of the mainline churches in Britain today would either agree with these statements, or even if they did agree with them, know how to put them into practice. It is not that the churches are not concerned for the poor; indeed, to the contrary, there is growing evidence that the churches are increasingly concerned for the poor and the causes of poverty as the number of the poor in Britain grows almost daily. When the Church of England report on Urban Priority Areas (UPAs) was first leaked and then published, it was abundantly clear that that Commission at least was very concerned about the poor — a concern which brought congratulations and condemnations almost equally down upon its head. Indeed, particularly in the first half of the Report, which is addressed to the Church itself, the Commission recognises the Gospel call to 'social and political action aimed at altering the circumstances which appear to cause poverty and distress',[7] and expresses the hope that 'we may expect to see in the Urban Priority Areas the emergence of a theology which would provide an authentic basis for a Christian critique of contemporary society'.[8] It even goes on to try to outline the sort of churches that it feels might be best to emerge from these UPAs; and reading it, one is inescapably reminded of the Church of Scotland reports already referred to, such as the Priorities of Mission report in the 1970s, and the Committee of Forty report at the end of the same decade, with their calls for smaller and larger units, neighbourhood worship-centres, and more lay leadership. Encouraging evidence is also to be found, in the Commission's comments on the relationship of the Church of England with other faiths as well as with other denominations, that the Commission at least does not believe the Christian church is to be for ever locked into confrontation with itself, let alone with other communities of faith, in today's multicultural society.

The Latin-American model

That said, it is difficult to avoid the impression that the Commission, despite the worthwhile and encouraging things it says about the need for the church in Urban Priority Areas to be local, outward-looking, participating and ecumenically-based, cannot see a church *of* the poor, as distinct from a church *for* the poor, emerging in England. Indeed, in a footnote to the Chapter on 'What Kind of Church?', the whole concept of 'base communities', the type of working-class model of the church which is growing so fast in Latin America today, is dismissed as being not directly transferable to the British context. The Commission points out, correctly, that the Latin American base churches are 'peasant, and pre-industrial, not concerned with upward social mobility, and have little reliance on outside professionals'.[9] These base communities may not be *directly* transferable to the British context, it is true; and the poor of our urban areas of multiple deprivation *are* different. They are secular, post-industrial, concerned with upward social mobility primarily because as a society we have sold our soul to consumerism, and dependent upon outside professionals, both lay and clerical, because the state and the church have made them so over centuries. To go on, as the Commission seems to do, to attempt to outline the sort of church that ought to be emerging in England without paying these base communities and their concerns a lot more attention, and without seeming to believe that the poor of England might, in fact, have a quite different approach and response to the Gospel from the one they believe they ought to have, places the Commission, and so the whole Report, in danger of coming under the same condemnation as the white American liberals of the Civil Rights struggle of the 1960s, who were so bluntly told by Martin Luther King, in his famous letter from Alabama Jail: 'In God's name, get out of our way!'

I write, let me hasten to add, as the equivalent of a white American liberal, whose whole approach is coloured by much of the same thinking as that of the members of the Commission. However, I have before me always the memory of the confrontation I had, in Gorbals just after Martin Luther King's assassination, with my black American Baptist friend, David Rice. Not surprisingly, David was devastated by King's tragic death, not only because of the profound personal and leadership loss of the whole Civil Rights movement. For David was being torn apart by the conflicting claims of his calling and his training as a Baptist Minister within a mainline American church, and his intense sense of identification with the Black Power Movement of the time. In the confusion of the days following the assassination, we had many a discussion about this. I asked him, I remember, to explain the Black Power Movement to me. I assumed, I said, that it meant that the blacks of America were claiming their fair share of power with the whites in the emerging American society for which they were struggling. I shall never forget the look of astonishment that came over his face, followed immediately by one of despair, as he replied: 'You're just the same as all the rest. Don't you realise that Black Power is nothing to do with sharing; it means the blacks on top at last!' To my instinctive cry of 'But that's not fair!' came back the harsh rejoinder, 'Has it been fair for the last 400 years?'.

Professor Jon Sobrino, in his book already mentioned tries, with the help of Moltman, to describe the sort of church that emerges when the poor 'become the subjects of their own history and not the objects', by referring to the traditional marks of the Church — One, Holy, Catholic and Apostolic. He discerns a move towards Unity in their commitment to the struggle for justice, seen as ultimately coming from God. He sees a move towards true Holiness amongst the poor, who see holiness 'as a matter of saving the world as the Servant did and as Jesus did, not by an exercise of power but from below: through poverty and solidarity with the poor, their cause and their destiny, their persecution and their martyrdom. The church thus recovers the deepest dimension of the holiness of Jesus, namely, his *kenosis* or self-emptying'.[10] He sees a move in the direction of true Catholicity, in that 'catholicity is not simply universalism nor the concrete application of universal principles but rather mutual responsibility within the church'.[11] As to Apostolicity, he quotes Moltman's words: 'Participation in the apostolic mission of Christ . . . leads inescapably into tribulation, contradiction and suffering . . . what we must learn is not that the church "has" a mission, but the very reverse: that the mission of Christ creates its own church'.[12] Sobrino writes out of the experience of the rapid growth, in Latin America, of the 'base communities' already mentioned; he, and other Latin American theologians, are rightly reflecting on what does indeed seem to be a 'new thing' that the Spirit is doing there amongst the poor and the dispossessed — and they are having their battles with their own hierarchy, as is to be expected, for what they are describing and reflecting upon, both theologically and ecclesiologically, does not always fit very easily into the patterns of thought and structure authorised by Rome, even after Vatican II. In Scotland, as in England, we are not in a position to describe and reflect in this way, for we do not see such a 'new thing' happening in our country and in the church here. Obviously, it would be contrary to all that has been said so far for us now to try to construct some sort of a model, or even a number of models, for what is being called, in some quarters, 'The Emerging Church'. Nor would it be helpful to analyse in detail the Latin American base communities in the hope that they will show us a model for ourselves; clearly, I do believe that they, and their theologians after them, are important for us as pointers to the way the Spirit can and does move in establishing the church of the poor in some parts of the world; but, as has already been said, they are not directly transferable, even if they might give us pause for thought and cause for hope.

Signposts
Nevertheless, such exploration and experimentation as has been done so far among the poor in our part of the world enables us to glimpse certain important signposts and even possibly ways ahead, and I end by mentioning some of them. These reflections, of course, will not be heard by the poor, who are to be our teachers, but if we are true students, then we might learn something of benefit to us all.

We may learn from the poor, first and foremost, about what it means to be truly human in the world. The broken, and crushing, nature of poverty, for one thing, calls in question our too easy acceptance of our relative affluence and comfortable standard of living — and cries out to us to be profoundly and continually disturbed until poverty is removed from our society. All efforts at confronting and removing poverty must be examined, and where possible supported by Christians, no matter how threatening such efforts may be to ourselves, and even if they are, as they mostly have been, from 'the top down' rather than 'from the bottom up'. Poverty, as we saw in an earlier chapter, is an offence to God precisely because it breaks and crushes human beings made in His image; and in our society today, poverty is breaking and crushing us all, not only the poor, for it is our humanity, as well as that of the poor, that is lessened and distorted as we allow poverty to exist in our midst.

The poor teach us also about community and solidarity, which is a lesson we also desperately need to learn again and again. We are not talking here about any 'ideal' of community — indeed, my experience is that community is not so much achieved as received, and received moreover normally through the heat of struggle and suffering. Fifty years ago, Dietrich Bonhoeffer warned us, in his little book *Life Together*, against loving our particular blueprint of community more than the real community in which we found ourselves, for that way lies idolatry and the destruction of true community, not its celebration. There is no 'ideal' community among the poor, but there is a community nevertheless; a profound sense of class solidarity, forged in struggle and oppression, still survives, threatened though it is by the cloying tentacles of consumerism and greed; that, and a realistic understanding of what can only be called 'good neighbourliness', which covers everything from the sense of 'street' care and concern to the celebration of life in pub and community hall, including the still surviving awareness of the value of the extended family group.

Among the poor, too, are lessons to be learnt for us all about the nature and the exercise of power. On the face of it, this may seem a paradoxical thing to say; for are not the poor the ones who are, above all, powerless in today's world? Yet power is not, of itself, a bad thing, any more than is conflict; both can be used for the betterment of humanity and for the glory of God and His Kingdom. Among the poor there is at least a recognition that power is not simply to be equated with muscle and privilege and the tradition of the past, but that it is really to do with freedom of choice, and with organisation, and with basic human needs like justice and right relationships and resources. It is not that the poor are, by nature, any more likely than the rest of us not to abuse power if and when they get it, but rather it is that the poor, largely because they have for so long been deprived of real power, have had to learn and learn, again and again, wherein real power resides. Hence, for instance, the continual struggle within the poor to retain solidarity of organisation and purpose, for only in that sort of solidarity do they find enough strength to pursue their proper needs for better conditions, including greater resources for their own use. Hence, also, the seriousness with which the poor take the question of income, not simply because they want more money (who does not?), but because they know that in our society, money buys you freedom of choice, buys you control over your own life and gives your children some hope of control over their own lives. And who are we, who have that in such great measure and have made such a mixed mess of it ourselves, to tell the poor, who do not have it, how they must use it if and when they get it? Hence, also, the involvement of many of the poor in politics; for politics is of course about resources and freedom and power; and there is very little understanding among the poor of the church's constant temerity about being involved in politics, which is seen simply as yet another example of the church's irrelevance to the real world.

The church has of course not made it any easier for the poor to see the connection between the coming of the Kingdom and political activity by preaching an individualistic version of the Gospel which really has more to do with an escape from the real world than a realistic involvement with it. There is no avoiding Ian Fraser's harsh condemnation of the church in this regard: we have 'let the good biblical word "reconciliation" . . . be watered down until it means "not causing trouble because we are Christians"'.

Lessons from the poor

We may learn from the poor, also, something of the true meaning of 'work' and 'occupation'. Again, they can teach us about this because they have been so deprived of it over the centuries, and here I am not just thinking of the disgraceful facts of unemployment which face us every day at the moment — they are bad enough — but I am also thinking of the way in which the poor have been treated even when work, as we traditionally know it, was available to them in any large measure. Then work was so often little more than slave labour, ill-controlled, unimaginatively organised, underpaid and primarily not for their benefit so much as for the benefit of the employers and their class. From them, then, we may learn that the true work that gives us our dignity, and our sense of participatory worth within the whole community, is not drudgery, and is certainly not the sort of short-term palliatives that are being handed out to the young and the long-term unemployed today, but is rather the properly rewarded opportunity to contribute whatever skill we have in the meaningful service of the whole commonwealth; and God knows we are light-years away from achieving that in Scotland today. Even to approach within sight of it, needs from us all — and therefore from the Christian church as well — determined and disciplined intellectual, political and industrial effort before which our shameful connivances and our conscience-saving temporary projects with the unemployed pale into insignificance.

What do the poor teach us about God? Certainly, they teach us that He is One, for no matter how determined the religions of the world are to make sure that their devotees practise apart and view their fellow-worshippers with profound suspicion and even fear, and no matter how willingly the poor accept the social and practical divisions which are thus insisted upon day in, day out, by the respective hierarchies, there is no getting away from their stubbornly held conviction that there is only One God, and that we shall all come before Him in the end, and that He will have time for each one of us. About Jesus the poor are far more uncertain, which is not surprising, considering how uncertain the message has been about Him and how confusing, over the centuries, especially from within the churches of the Reformation. (Protestants envy Catholics their certainty, their consistency, and their controlled authoritative religion — while protesting at all these things should they ever become too obvious within their own religion!) As for actually practising religion together, rather than in separate vacuum-sealed worship centres and schools, there is among the poor an almost wistful longing that this could be done — a gut conviction that this ought to be done — but a resigned acceptance that this cannot be done. Again this is hardly surprising for, at least as far as the Church of Scotland and Roman Catholic leadership is concerned, there is no evidence that either of the respective hierarchies really believe that it will be done, in spite of their oft-repeated statements to the contrary. The ecumenical process, if we may call it that, moves along the wrong axis anyway. It is concerned, it seems, more to find some sort of common ground on which all parties can stand and somehow co-operate, when what it should be doing is engaging, often painfully and in real and deep (but hopefully courteous) conflict, at points of the world's confusion, division and despair; as Ian Fraser says, 'a church at peace within itself in a world of disorder is a testimony against the Gospel'.

All these things which the poor may have to teach us — never simply, never consistently, but real lessons nonetheless — relate, when you come to think of it, very much to the message of Jesus and His Kingdom of God. Humanity, poverty and its offensiveness to human worth, community and solidarity, the nature and the exercise of power, the nature and meaning of conflict and suffering, the meaning of work, and the one-ness and basic love of God — these are central themes of the Gospel. The poor do not, on the whole, recognise them within the church, for the simple yet terrifying reason that they are not recognisably there. Or rather, they are not there for them to see. They may be spoken of in the church, chiefly from the pulpit, but they are not available for the poor to see and touch and feel and share in, because they are not in the main incarnate in the life of the church on the street, in the tenement, in pub and bingo queue and football terracing. 'The Word made Flesh', cries the poet, 'is thus made Word again'. What then must we do? And by 'we' I mean quite specifically the remnant that is the institutional church still left near to the poor; small in numbers and ever decreasing; burdened with financial and fabric anxieties; regarded as a problem by the hierarchies; and yet often, in the midst of uncertainty and difficulty and inner doubts and lack of confidence, managing to maintain at least a sort of caring and worshipping presence in the areas of multiple deprivation in our cities and towns. Certainly what we do not need is for those not in our situation to make us feel even more inadequate than we do already, by forever summoning us to greater efforts of evangelism and piety which, it must be said, often sound like little more than the sugar on the bitter pills of the demands for more and more money. Nor will it help for us to go on assuming that the answer is to be found in new ways of tempting the poor to get out of their beds at 11.00 *am* on a Sunday morning, or to prise them away from the TV at 7.30 *pm* on a Monday evening. The activities of the institutional church at these and other times during the week are, and I imagine will always be, meaningful for a proportion of the population of Scotland — I suspect for little more than ten per cent of it today. They cannot claim to be the only, or even, the best vessels for the Gospel today, or any day, and to do them well, as well as we possibly can, is not the same thing as going on to assume that they will therefore work for those outside the church. Indeed, to bring the outsiders into the institutional church as it is at present constituted, even if we could, would be to run the risk, always allowing for the maverick Spirit of God, of turning them into carbon copies of ourselves.

Making room

One thing we can do, it seems to me, is to make room, both in our thinking and in our strategy, for a parallel church to appear. For too long we seem to have assumed, quite uncritically, that we know what form the church ought to take everywhere, even among the poor, as far as the mainline churches are concerned; all our efforts, such as they have been, have been directed to reform and renewal of what is basically the same structure and activities in the hope that it will eventually work as it did before. As we have seen, this is both unrealistic and disobedient, and therefore ought to be departed from. What might be required now, is for a few people, preferably members of the local congregation, to agree to enter upon a sustained and long-term exercise in re-education and engagement alongside the poor of their area, with the clear purpose, not of bringing the poor eventually back into the congregation as they have known it, but rather of letting the Spirit work through them, and through their neighbours, so that a new thing might emerge. Obviously, the difficulties of such an exercise are immense. Such a nucleus, for instance, would need to be locally based, and therefore exposed to all the realities of the life of the poor — but at the same time, they would be exposed to their own inner doubts and limitations, and to the very real anxieties of their fellow church-members, who might see them as break-away cliques, intent only on destroying the fragile unity of the congregation already under threat. Further, if the nucleus were really open to the life of the poor, and began to reflect some of their concerns and insights in their common life as Christians, it seems likely that these would be seen as threatening the activities and practices of the traditional churches. Long-held prejudices might disappear, long-accepted barriers might begin to dissolve, and the wind that might begin to blow, which to some might appear to be the wind of the Spirit, to others might seem to be the wind of Auld Nick himself. Progress, if there were any, would of necessity have to be slow, for there is a vast amount of lost ground to be made up. The gap between the church and the poor is huge, but so also, at times, is the gap between the ordinary church member and the Gospel of Jesus and His Kingdom. The institutional church's consuming desire for results, for statistics, for returns, is never far away. Perhaps most subtly threatening of all, is the church's habit of treating any attempt at 'a new thing' as simply another experiment, interesting while it lasts, but of little real importance as far as the mission of the church is concerned. But what we are suggesting here is not yet another experiment; it is rather an exercise in exploration and church extension from within, from the bottom up, with no preconceived assumptions as to the shape of what will emerge, if by the grace of God something does begin to emerge at all.

There are precedents for such an exercise, although you have to dig pretty deep to find them. In the Middle Ages, in the days of first Catholic and then Protestant and Catholic Christendom in Europe, the mainline churches dealt with any such experiments — for example, the Albigensians and the Waldensians — by persecution, for they could not afford to let them survive. In the seventeenth century, Christians driven to seeking alternatives to the mainline churches had to emigrate to the New World, but there are no New Worlds available to us at the moment. In England, the Wesleyans and the Salvationists, desperate to stay in touch with the mainline churches while they sought to reach the poor of the Industrial Revolution, were also forced out, and in many cases were forced also by their own inner weaknesses to conform to the very pattern they had seen as already having failed. In our own century, parallel structures have been tried here and there. One thinks of the German Industrial Missioner, Horst Symanowski, trying to develop a parallel structure for the new industrial workers and their families in post-war Germany, even to the extent of coming to terms with the continental shift-system and developing a congregation which worshipped only every third or fourth week-end. In Scotland today, the Iona Community is currently developing small Columban Houses of mainly young people, often disenchanted with the practice of the mainline churches in which they have been brought up, living together in community in flats and tenements, and trying to discover the sort of obedience, in action and in worship and in life-style, that God wants for them in todays's world.

Can the church today allow such an exercise to happen alongside its more traditional activities? Can the hierarchies allow it — even more questionable, can local congregations allow it — even if, as might conceivably happen, it begins to produce a sort of church which in many respects develops a quite different style of worship, activity and piety from the traditional forms? One has to pose the ultimate question: can the church allow such an exercise, and not just allow it but encourage it, even if it produces confusion and failure and conflict, and disturbs the peace of the church — or even if it actually begins to replace the church as we have known it for so long?

No-one can answer these questions until it is tried. If and when it is tried, it will not necessarily save the church. It might — just might — serve the cause of the Gospel of Jesus Christ and His Kingdom. It might — just might — bring healing to a broken world. It might — just might — be Good News to the Poor.

References

1 Sobrino (1985), p85f.
2 Ward (1949), p111.
3 Ward (1949), p111f.
4 Fraser (1975), pp127–129.
5 de Santa Ana (1977), p21.
6 Sobrino (1985), p92f.
7 Church of England (1985), p48.
8 Church of England (1985), p64.
9 Church of England (1985), p80.
10 Sobrino (1985), p109.
11 Sobrino (1985), p115.
12 Sobrino (1985), p117.

Bibliography

Allan, Tom (1954) *The Face of My Parish*, SCM Press, London, reissued 1984 by Loudoun Publications, Glasgow.

Barry, F R (1969) *Secular and Supernatural*, SCM Press, London.

Brierley, Peter and Macdonald, Fergus (1985) *Prospects for Scotland*, The National Bible Society of Scotland, Edinburgh, and MARC Europe, Bromley.

Brown, Gordon and Cook, Robin, (Eds) (1983) *Scotland: The Real Divide*, Mainstream Publishing, Edinburgh.

Brown, Stewart J (1982) *Thomas Chalmers and the Godly Commonwealth*, Open University Press, Milton Keynes.

Campbell, Calum (1986) *The Making of a Clydeside Working Class*, Communist Party History Group Publications.

Christian Action (1965) *The Gorbals 1965*, Christian Action, London.

Church of England (1985) *Faith in the City*: the Report of the Archbishop of Canterbury's Commission on Urban Priority Areas, Church House Publishing, London.

Church of Scotland (1971) *Report of the Special Commission on Priorities of Mission in Scotland in the 1970s*, Church of Scotland, Edinburgh.

Church of Scotland (1978) *People with a Purpose: The 40 File*, Church of Scotland, Edinburgh.

Church of Scotland (1980) *Into the Eighties: Report of the Joint Working Party on a Programme for Action*, Church of Scotland, Edinburgh.

Donnison, David (1982) *The Politics of Poverty*, Martin Robertson, Oxford.

Edwards, David L, (Ed) (1961) *Priests and Workers: An Anglo-French Discussion*, SCM Press, London.

Ferguson, Ron (1979) *Geoff: The Life of Geoffrey M Shaw*, Famedram Publishers, Gartocharn.

Fraser, Ian M (1975) *The Fire Runs*, SCM Press, London.

Galloway, Allan D (1967) *Faith in a Changing Culture: The Kerr Lectures 1966*, George Allen and Unwin, London.

Garbett, Cyril (1952) *In an Age of Revolution*, Hodder and Stoughton, London.

Godfrey, John and Goldie, Ella (1978) *Chartism and Paisley*, Local History Archives Project, Jordanhill College, Glasgow.

Johnston, Tom (1946) *The History of the Working Classes in Scotland*, Glasgow Unity Publishing.

Kenrick, Bruce (1962) *Come Out the Wilderness*, Harper and Brothers, New York.

McIntyre, Alasdair (1967) *Secularisation and Moral Change: The Riddell Memorial Lectures*, Oxford University Press.

Macleod, George F (1936) *Are Not the Churchless Millions Partly the Church's Fault?*, Church of Scotland, Edinburgh.

Macleod, George F (1957) *Bombs and Bishops*, Iona Community, Glasgow.

Mcleod, Hugh (1974) *Class and Religion in the Late Victorian City*, Croom Helm, London.

Michonneau, Abbé (1949) *Revolution in a City Parish*, Blackfriars, London.

Middlemas, R K (1965) *The Clydesiders*, Hutchinson, London.

Morton, Ralph and Gibbs, Mark (1964) *God's Frozen People*, Fontana Books, London.

Morton, Ralph and Gibbs, Mark (1971) *God's Lively People*, Fontana Books, London.

Perrin, Henri (1947) *Priest-Workman in Germany*, Sheed and Ward, London.

Robinson, J A T (1965) *The New Reformation?*, SCM Press, London.

de Santa Ana, Julio (1977) *Good News to the Poor*, World Council of Churches, Geneva.

de Santa Ana, Julio, (Ed) (1978) *Separation without Hope?*, World Council of Churches, Geneva.

de Santa Ana, Julio (1979) *Towards a Church of the Poor*, World Council of Churches, Geneva.

Schwiezer, E (1961) *Church Order in the New Testament*, SCM Press, London.

Sissons, Peter (1973) *The Social Significance of Church Membership in the Burgh of Falkirk*, Church of Scotland, Edinburgh.

Smout, T C (1986) *A Century of the Scottish People, 1830-1950*, Collins, London.

Sobrino, Jon (1985) *The True Church and the Poor*, translated by Matthew J O'Connell, SCM Press, London.

Southcott, E W (1956) *The Parish Comes Alive*, A R Mowbray, London.

Thompson, E P (1977) *William Morris, Romantic to Revolutionary*, Merlin Press, London.

Thompson, Paul (1967) *Socialists, Liberals and Labour: The Struggle for London*, Routledge and Kegan Paul, Toronto.

United Presbyterian Church (1964) *The City — God's Gift to the Church*, Board of National Mission of the United Presbyterian Church in the USA, New York.

Ward, Maisie (1949) *France Pagan? The Mission of Abbé Godin*, Sheed and Ward, London.

Williams, Colin (1963) *Where in the World*, National Council of Churches of Christ in the USA, New York.

World Council of Churches (1967) *The Church for Others and the Church for the World: A Quest for Structures for Missionary Congregations*, Department of Studies in Evangelism, World Council of Churches, Geneva.